P·R·E·A·C·H·I·N·G

MAN & METHOD

P·R·E·A·C·H·I·N·G

MAN & METHOD

An Intensive Study
Of the Preparation
And Delivery of Sermons

Second Edition, Revised and Enlarged

STAFFORD

NORTH

RESOURCE □
PUBLICATIONS
202 S. Locust
Searcy, AR 72143

ISBN: 0-945441-18-5

ALL SCRIPTURE QUOTATIONS are from The Holy Bible,
the American Standard Edition of the Revised Bible, 1901.

DEDICATION

To JoAnne

A preacher who has the blessing of a faithful wife will find his life richer, his ministry more productive, his successes sweeter, his problems shared, and his prospect of heaven increased. I say this because it is what JoAnne has meant to me.

In Memory

Glenda Stamper, a beloved Christian lady, was struck with cancer while she was working as my secretary on the revision of this book. While unable to do regular work, she persisted in bringing this manuscript almost to completion. This edition is presented to the public in memory of Glenda's dedication and generous spirit.

Contents

Preface

If the doctor whose knife delicately removes a portion of the brain must approach his work with thorough knowledge, intensive training and extreme seriousness, what must be the approach of the preacher who operates on the *soul*, and whose effects must be weighed on a scale of eternal values? If you are a preacher or wish to preach, you have chosen a work so important that no human being can calculate its vast significance. James expressed it well in saying, "Be not many of you teachers, my brethren, knowing that we shall receive the heavier judgment" (James 3:1). Let no one undertake a life of preaching without thought and prayer, but once the decision to preach is made or the "call" accepted, then *let no effort be spared in making preparation.*

This book is written as a guide to studying the *pulpit work* of the preacher. The approach is (1) *to consider the biblical view of the preacher* and (2) *to apply the principles of effective speaking to sermon preparation and delivery.* While the approach assumes that the student has had some study in public speaking, the principles of public address are reviewed and applied specifically to the preaching situation. For some, this book will be a good personal review of what they have studied earlier. For others it will be a class textbook.

For those studying in a classroom situation, the delivery of sermons offers the opportunity to practice the principles. In addition, writing affords the student an opportunity to develop

9

exactness and accuracy in composition since improvement in this area will carry over to speaking ability.

This study is directed toward *specific objectives*:

First, the student can *demonstrate on a written examination* that he has mastered the *information* given him on certain principles of preaching as he does the following:

1. Defines preaching and homiletics (Chapter 1).

2. Briefly recounts the history of preaching (Chapter 1).

3. Explains the immediate and long-range aims of preaching and the achievement of them (Chapter 1).

4. Reviews the five canons of classical rhetoric (Chapter 1).

5. Lists and explains the personal qualities of the preacher (Chapter 2).

6. Describes the process of preparation for a sermon (Chapter 3).

7. Explains the needs of an audience in terms of the struggle between the physical and spiritual, satisfying inborn drives, and solving emotional problems (Chapter 4).

8. Explains how to make a sermon biblical, interesting, practical, and significant (Chapter 4).

9. Lists and explains the inborn drives and describes their use by the preacher (Chapter 4).

10. Discusses the four types of sermon purposes (Chapter 5).

11. Analyzes the organization of a sermon given him orally or in print and identifies the type according to classifications given him (Chapter 6).

12. Classifies examples of supporting material into types given him (Chapter 7).

13. Classifies examples of reasoning and recognizes their validity or fallacy (Chapter 7).

14. Explains the levels of emotional appeal (Chapter 7).

15. Classifies appeals to action according to the drive they satisfy (Chapter 7).

16. Describes the qualities of style a preacher should seek

and identifies the use of figures of speech (Chapter 8).

17. Explains the use of both voice and body in preaching (Chapter 9).

Second, the student can *demonstrate through written assignments* done for class his *skill* in sermon preparation as he does the following:

1. Determines the purpose and subject sentence for a sermon being designed to meet a given situation and explains how this choice will meet the needs of the audience—"So what?" (Chapter 4).

2. Prepares a sermon outline according to the style given him (Chapters 3, 6).

3. Prepares a sermon outline on any of the sermon patterns given him (Chapter 6).

4. Designs effective introductions, transitions, and conclusions (Chapter 6).

5. Locates and/or devises effective support to clarify, interest, convince, or move (Chapter 7).

6. Develops appeals to actions based on various drives and emotions (Chapter 7).

7. Words a sermon to exhibit the qualities of clarity, correctness, vividness, and forcefulness (Chapter 8).

Third, the student can *prepare and deliver a sermon* which meets the standards of subject selection, organization, use of supporting material, style, and use of voice and body suggested in the text.

In addition to reading the text and class discussion, other possible assignments for the student include the following:

1. Answer in writing the discussion questions with Chapters 1, 2, and 4 to be handed in at the time of class discussion of the chapter. Answers should reflect some research in the books and articles on preaching. Footnotes and references, in proper form, should accompany each paper submitted on the discussion questions.

2. Prepare and deliver in class at least four sermons assigned in connection with various units. These should be new

sermons, not ones used before.

3. Keep a sermon subject and illustration file. These may be on cards or in a loose-leaf notebook. He should carry with him at all times a note card and pen to put down ideas which occur to him. He should get the homiletic habit. Samples of this file will be reviewed by the instructor at the end of the semester.

4. In connection with Chapter 6, turn in ten brief sermon outlines containing the purpose, subject sentence, text, and main headings of the body from an assigned chapter in the Bible. These will demonstrate various types of sermons and sermon plans.

5. In connection with Chapters 4, 5, and 6, analyze some congregation and work out short outlines of two sermons a week for six weeks which will be aimed at the needs of the group. For these sermons, the student should list the purpose, subject sentence, text, and main points of the body.

Other specific assignments are listed with each chapter.

Teachers using this book as a text for a class should have sufficient assignments that the students use the principles and practices encouraged here enough that they become well established in their thought patterns. Assignments should, of course, be carefully critiqued.

Students in this book are addressed in the masculine even though the author recognizes that women who can speak well are also needed in the church today. While the author considers the Scriptures to assign differing roles to men and women, he believes we need more women who can speak well. Since most of the students in homiletics classes, however, will be men and because of the awkwardness in English in including both sexes, he has used masculine pronouns to include those of either sex who are studying this subject.

1 | The Role Of the Preacher

"Preach the word" — 2 Timothy 4:2

INTRODUCTION

In 490 B.C., Darius, King of Persia, directed his vast armada over the Aegean Sea toward Marathon, a few miles northeast of Athens. When the Athenians learned they were to be attacked, they determined to call on the neighboring Spartans to forget their past disputes and to help them protect Greece from the Persians. In less than forty-eight hours Pheidippides ran the hundred or more miles to Sparta and convinced the Spartans to join in the fight. Two thousand Spartan soldiers left immediately.

All Americans are familiar with the story of Paul Revere, who, on the night of April 18, 1775, rode over the New England countryside to warn that the British troops under General Gage were on the way to Lexington.

We honor and praise those who, with great courage, carried a message of importance with such urgency. We laud them because they understood their mission and accomplished it with dispatch.

With an even greater sense of urgency, the apostles received Jesus' words, "Go into all the world and preach the gospel unto every creature" (Mark 16:15). When the Jewish authorities charged them not to speak in the name of Jesus, they replied, "We must obey God rather than men" (Acts 5:42). The zeal of the apostles was so contagious that Luke records, "They therefore that were scattered abroad went everywhere preaching the word" (Acts 8:4).

Paul even declared that he was a "slave" in bondage to preaching the gospel, to bringing the good news of the gospel to lost souls (Romans 1:14-15). To the Corinthians he wrote: "Woe is unto me, if I preach not the gospel" (1 Corinthians 9:16). No wonder he charged his convert, Timothy, "Preach the word; be urgent in season, out of season; reprove, rebuke, exhort, with all longsuffering and teaching" (2 Timothy 4:2).

Compared with this, the messages of Pheidippides and Paul Revere shrink to nothing, for here, indeed, is *the world's greatest responsibility.*

No matter how great the grace of God or how great the sacrifice of Jesus, however, these are to no avail until they are known to the sinner. This is always a human responsibility. Never in the New Testament record did God directly tell a sinner what to do to obtain salvation through Christ. Even in the cases of Cornelius, Saul, and the Ethiopian where God aided directly in getting the message to them, God used a human being to tell the message of salvation. As Paul wrote, "How then shall they call on him in whom they have not believed? and how shall they believe in whom they have not heard? and how shall they hear without a preacher?" (Romans 10:14). Only through the human agency, then, does God make His great offer of salvation known around the world, and, in this study, we are especially concerned with public proclamation as a means of fulfilling this responsibility to make disciples of all nations.

"But," someone objects, "doesn't the Bible itself declare that preaching is foolishness? How can foolishness occupy such an important place?" In 1 Corinthians 1:21 Paul indeed wrote: "It was God's good pleasure through the foolishness of the preaching to save them that believe." The context makes it clear, as does the Greek construction, however, that he here refers to the content of the preaching as "foolish," not to the act of preaching. He continues: "But we preach Christ crucified, unto Jews a stumbling block and unto Gentiles foolishness." The message is what they considered foolish, not the act of public speaking. If speaking well were foolish, it would not be employed by those who seek success in everything from politics to romance.

Preaching, then, is the most vital role among men, for he who would preach becomes a messenger of God, a channel through which can flow the message of God, a harp tuned to the truth and playing the strain sung by angels, "Peace on earth, good will to men."

Discussion Question: Is public proclamation of the gospel as important today as it was in the first century?

PREACHING AND HOMILETICS DEFINED

The best known definition of preaching was given by Phillips Brooks: "Preaching is the communication of truth by man to men. It has in it two essential elements—truth and personality."[1] An understanding of this definition reveals much regarding the almost incomprehensibly great responsibility of the preacher.

"Communication" suggests that preaching involves transmitting an idea from the mind of the sender to the mind of the receiver. Preaching is not the art of speaking the message of God; rather, it is the act of getting a listener to comprehend the message of God for him and to do something about it. The essence of preaching, then, is speaking so that listeners receive and act. This book seeks to help preachers to do this effectively.

"Truth," in Brooks' definition, implies that the *content* of preaching must be consistent with the Word of God. Anything more or less than the "oracles of God" is not true preaching. How great an obligation lies on the preacher to convey *God's*

---

[1]Phillips Brooks, *Lectures on Preaching* (Grand Rapids: Zondervan Publishing House, n.d.), 5.

message and *not* his own. The many New Testament passages that distinguish between the "false" and the "true" emphasize the vital necessity for the preacher to study with an open mind so he may "preach the word."

With the phrase, "by man to men," Brooks focuses attention on the *human element* in preaching. God intended for the preacher to add *something* to the message—not to change the meaning but to *add the power of the preacher's own experience, personality, and testimony.*

So God shines His truth like the sunlight upon the world, but all the people are inside where the sunshine cannot be seen. The preacher is the window which permits the truth to shine to the people groping blindly within.

This is not to say, of course, that one cannot learn the truth directly from the written Word with no spoken word employed, for such can and has taken place. For the common man, however, such occasions are rare, for not many become interested enough to read carefully for themselves until they have been encouraged and taught by some Christian, usually a preacher or one whom a preacher has encouraged. It is in this way, then, that the preacher becomes the pane through which God's light reaches mankind in general today.

If the preacher, as a window pane, is colored by prejudice, the people receive an imperfect light. If the preacher speaks with uncertainty when immediate direction is required, the light is dim and inadequate. If the preacher transmits his message obscurely without adequate preparation and without clarity in thought and expression, those in darkness remain there.

The preacher, then, must never distort or change the message of God. He must keep the focus on Jesus Christ, not on himself; he must speak on topics from God, not man. In short, he must clarify the way to heaven. While his own example and faith can help the message move from heart to heart, the preacher must communicate God's saving Word.

Now, what is homiletics? The purpose of homiletics is to assist the preacher in transmitting the message of God in the manner which will reveal the greatest amount of illuminating truth. We may, therefore, define homiletics as *the science of applying the principles of effective public speaking to the religious address; it is the art of applying the truth of God to the needs of men.*

Homiletics is a "science" because it is based on *principles which contribute to the success of speakers.* These principles have been recognized since the days of Aristotle and Plato and are rooted in the nature of human thought. At the same time, there is much in preaching that partakes of *"art."* The preacher needs to have a poetic imagination and must use those elements of all art such as balance, emphasis, form, unity, and climax. This book, then, is a discussion of the science and art of preaching.

Discussion Questions: How does preaching differ from any other form of public speaking such as a manager speaking to his employees? To what extent does a preacher rely on himself and to what extent upon God?

A BRIEF HISTORY OF PREACHING

History is replete with the record of those who faithfully ministered the message of God to their fellow creatures. Enoch (Jude 1) prophesied; Noah was a preacher of God's righteousness (2 Peter 2:5); Moses delivered three lengthy addresses which are recorded in Deuteronomy; Joshua and Samuel spoke the words of God to the people. The prophets—the word means *proclaimer* or *revealer* and not merely foreteller—burned with zeal for the Lord and spoke with force, vigor and striking illustration their "thus saith the Lord."

John the Baptist was so popular in his day that "all Jerusalem and Judea" came to his "revival," and Jesus Himself was a preacher as well as a teacher, counselor, and philosopher.

The Holy Spirit used many voices during the infancy of the church: Peter, bold and positive; Stephen, clear and courageous; Paul, logical and zealous. These and an army of others carried the battle to the enemy and won with the unsheathed Sword of the Spirit, "speaking as the Spirit gave them utterance." These were, for the most part, unlearned and untrained in the art of rhetoric, but the Lord found in them those natural qualities of faith, sincerity, vigor, and earnestness which He

utilized in delivering His message. They truly were ambassa-
dors of God, for the Lord guided them in their speaking even as
He had promised (Matthew 10:14; John 14:26; 16:13).

Following these came others who were equally devoted and
zealous, but who found their message, not directly from the
Spirit Himself, but from the first generation Christians who had
written with their pens dipped in the ink of inspiration. By the
fourth century, pulpit oratory had achieved a high degree of
excellence for it was during this post-Nicene era that: (1)
Augustine (A.D. 354-430), a converted rhetorician, was applying Ciceronian rhetoric to Christian preaching; (2) that *Ambrose*
(A.D. 340-397), from his pulpit in Milan, was ably defending
against the "Arian heresy"; and (3) *Chrysostom* (A.D. 347-
407), called "The Golden-Mouthed," was eloquently preaching
in Antioch and Constantinople.

From this zenith, however, there was a rapid decline into the
darkness of the middle ages when little notable preaching was
done. Many contend that the preaching during this age was
ineffective because it depended less and less on the Scriptures
and more and more on the views of councils and theologians.
Substantiating this belief is the fact that with the Reformation
Movement came a return to greater preaching. All the great
reformers—Luther, Calvin, Knox, Wesley, Savonarola—made
use of preaching to expound their views and stir their followers.
These were followed by a second and third generation of
pulpiteers such as Jonathan Edwards (1703-58) and George
Whitefield (1714-70), who led the way in the American "Great
Awakening" of the late eighteenth century; Henry Ward Beecher
(1813-87) and Phillips Brooks (1835-93) who swayed thou-
sands in America during the nineteenth century; and Alexander
Campbell (1788-1866), Walter Scott (1796-1861), and Barton
W. Stone (1772-1844) who led in beginning the Restoration
Movement in America. In England, meanwhile, Frederick W.
Robertson (1816-53), Charles Spurgeon (1834-92), and Alex-
ander Maclaren (1826-1910) were delivering sermons to throngs.

Today, of course, many have become widely known as
effective spokesmen. Some of these have made extensive use of
radio and television as well as the printed page. Each person

studying to be a public proclaimer should select several effective preachers for observation. No one should copy the style of another, for each must be "his own man" according to his own personality and background; yet, each can learn from both the strong and weak points of others. A study of this book will give many points to consider in learning from others.

THE AIM OF PREACHING

As this procession of preachers passes in review, certain observations become evident. *Greatness in preaching combines a sense of urgency for the needs of mankind with the Spirit-revealed message of God for these needs.* Great preaching, even good preaching, demands an understanding of both human needs and divine remedies.

From these preachers one can discover, too, the fundamental function of the preacher: *to develop men spiritually so they may some day reach heaven.* To those who have been born of the water and the Spirit, he must provide direction to a *stronger and deeper spirituality.* The preacher who conceives of his role as that of ministering primarily to physical and social needs, may be of some help to his congregation, but as Paul indicated to Timothy, "Bodily exercise is profitable for a little; but godliness is profitable for all things, having promise of the life which now is, and of that which is to come" (1 Timothy 4:8). He who saves bodies does *well*; he who saves minds does *better*; but he who saves souls does *best*.

What can the preacher do and how can he spend his time in order to edify the spirits in his congregation? Should the preacher be a public speaker, a private teacher, a counselor, a visitor, an administrator, a secretary, a janitor, or all of these? No one, of course, can outline exactly how every preacher in every congregation should spend his hours, but a few observations can be of value.

If a preacher's primary goal is to assist in the spiritual development of individuals, *his primary means for achieving this goal must be through teaching and inspiring.* Some of this he does through his exemplary life; some through his personal contact with the members; and some through his classroom teaching. *But his primary method for teaching and inspiring should be his utterances from the pulpit,* and it is to this work that he should devote the largest part of his time.

In the late twentieth century, there has been a tendency to regard pulpit proclamation as having a diminishing importance. A special series by a visiting evangelist, for example, does not turn out the community as it often did in pre-television days. And, because of the degrading portrayal of preaching in television and movies along with the scandals associated with some well-known preachers, public opinion of the ministry is at an all-time low.

Yet, there is no doubt that public proclamation is still a most effective means for affecting opinions, beliefs, and actions. An effective speaker can inspire and motivate in ways nothing else can match. Public officials, such as presidents, congressmen, and governors, find it essential; no one running for public office at any level would dare refuse to make public speeches; business organizations, education, and even the legal and medical professions find public presentations to be critical to achieving their ends.

The experience in churches is also clear. Congregations with an effective spokesman in the pulpit find their members more active and their outreach more effective than those whose preacher cannot hold attention or present a well-organized discourse. Those who would be public proclaimers, then, must give to sermon preparation and delivery a high priority. They must learn well the principles that undergird effective preaching and must develop the skills it requires. Then, when they are on the job, they must continue to give this part of their work a high priority.

Good preaching, even by an effective speaker, requires both extensive specific preparation and personal spiritual growth. Without taking time for both of these, a minister will not long continue to be able to move audiences effectively.

The preacher must, therefore, devote time to study, meditation, and prayer. He must be a person of ever-increasing depth of soul and character, and one of continually-increasing insights and information. When he allows other matters to encroach on the time required for his own development, he is allowing a cancerous growth which will eventually kill his effectiveness.

A careful study of lives of the best preachers over the years will confirm that for continuing service to a congregation, a preacher must be engaged in a constant program of personal development. In our day of speed, rush, and a constant "too busy" sign on the door, it is difficult, oftentimes, for the preacher to convince first himself, then others, that his own meditation is fundamental to the congregation. A look at great preachers, however, should be convincing. Alexander Campbell, for example, arose at 3:00 a.m. to study and write without interruption before breakfast.[2] Walter Scott studied the four gospels so carefully and had his students study them so carefully, that they all memorized these four books of the New Testament—in Greek.[3] Jonathan Edwards read very widely in books ranging from history and novels through commentaries and encyclopedias to trigonometry and midwifery.[4] Theodore Parker, likewise, had a library of 20,000 volumes and in answer to the question of what he read, one biographer answered, "Everything."[5]

Now this is not to say that the preacher should remove himself from his people or that he should not visit, counsel, and perhaps on occasion, even do physical labor for the church. Such is necessary for him to assess properly the needs and condition of those to whom he owes his efforts. The congregation must sense, however, a preacher's principal task is to speak from the pulpit for the purpose of stimulating spiritual development and to this he must devote himself unstintingly.

---

[2]Robert Richardson, *Memoirs of Alexander Campbell* (Cincinnati: Standard Publishing Co., 1897), II, 300.

[3]Ibid., I, 509.

[4]Orville A. Hitchcock, "Jonathan Edwards," *History and Criticism of American Public Address*, ed. William Norwood Brigance (New York: McGraw-Hill Book Co., Inc., 1943), I, 219.

[5]Roy C. McCall, "Theodore Parker," *History and Criticism of American Public Address*, ed. William Norwood Brigance (New York: McGraw-Hill Book Co., 1943), I, 240.

In this work, a preacher must seek both an immediate and a long-range response. There will be times when he seeks a goal of immediate action: an increased offering, improvement in the worship by singing, a conversion, an agreement on a particular point of doctrine. But in many other cases, the preacher will be seeking a goal of long-range spiritual growth. As in the case of physical exercise, such growth is discernible only after many occasions. He may, for example, teach on faith, patience, and zeal as part of his continuing effort to develop character. On other occasions he will preach on salvation, atonement, the resurrection, and judgment as part of his long-range plan for inculcating within his hearers an understanding of God's plan for reconciling man. Still other sermons will treat lasciviousness, covetousness, modesty, marriage, honesty, drunkenness, and citizenship in order to build an understanding of moral principles and the ability to discriminate between right and wrong. On such occasions the preacher is not seeking an immediate response so much as he is attempting to build a system of values and concepts—building blocks in a spiritual house.

The human mind is a marvelous and wonderful instrument. Every action, every idea, every thought of a person is recorded in our conscious or subconscious memory. When we are making a decision or producing communication, all those actions, ideas, and thoughts from our past come into play as the decision is being made. In a way not unlike a computer operator, the preacher is helping his congregation to store information in preparation for decisions and actions which will soon come upon them. They are often strongly influenced by sermons they no longer consciously recall.

In order to move the members of his congregation and others to a *higher spiritual plane,* the preacher must put forth all the effort he can. The congregation must perceive of him as a *hard worker* or else they will not take him seriously when he speaks of how important spiritual matters are. He should set as a rule of thumb to spend at least forty hours a week in church work *beyond* the hours he expects a member of his congregation to spend in religious service. If, for example, he expects one of his members to work forty hours a week as a carpenter and then to attend services and do personal work another four or five hours a week, the preacher should do no less.

Of course, the minister must know his own nature. While some are tempted to do too little, others are tempted to do too much. Some seek to delegate everything they can; others to delegate nothing. The preacher should follow his own advice: he will tell a father, spend some time with the children; he will tell another, take a little time for recreation; he will advise another, you need to give more time to the Lord. He may well apply such counsel to himself.

Discussion Questions: What will tend to draw a preacher away from what should be his main focus? Who are some effective preachers today and why are they effective?

THE PREACHER'S USE OF RHETORIC

As a part of this study of the role of the preacher, it will be helpful to see the connection between a preacher's use of public presentation to achieve spiritual ends and the *art of rhetoric*.

The word "rhetoric" was used in the ancient world to describe "persuasive discourse," whether written or spoken. Such noted philosophers as Plato, Aristotle, and Cicero gave much attention to those principles one should follow who desired to move men to belief or action. Paul appears to take note of those "sophists" who took these principles to the extreme when he separates himself from those who used "excellency of speech" (1 Corinthians 2:1). Certainly no preacher today should base his approach to his listeners on "flowery words" or "clever reasoning."

At the same time, however, Paul employed many of the techniques of the good speaker in his sermons: identification with his audience, careful use of evidence, effective organization of ideas, moving from points of agreement to points of disagreement, urgency in delivery, and many others.

The preacher, then, can learn many useful lessons from the rhetorician. Since the basis of the principles of rhetoric lies in human nature, even those principles written by Plato and Aristotle three or four centuries before the birth of Christ are still valid. Since frequent reference to them will be made throughout this book, a brief overview of them will be helpful at the outset.

Ancient rhetoricians divided effective speaking into five topics (canons) with each having associated with it many suggestions for good speaking:

1. INVENTION—the process of gathering and planning the use of the materials and ideas to move the audience. These materials should be chosen to utilize the three basic types of appeals to the audience: (1) *Logical Appeals* (λόγος)—based on evidence and reasoning, (2) *Emotional Appeals* (πάθος)—based on drives and feelings, (3) *Ethical Appeals* (ἦθος)—based on the character, personality, experience, and reputation of the speaker.

2. DISPOSITION—organizing and arranging the materials in the best way to achieve the purpose of the speaker.

3. STYLE—the selection and arrangement of words to convey the message in the most effective way.

4. MEMORY—remembering the message to be spoken.

5. DELIVERY—the use of voice and body to present the message to the audience with the greatest impact.

As reference is made throughout this book to the ancient canons of rhetoric, a recollection of this outline will be helpful.

CONCLUSION

The preacher, then, is a spokesman for God. He must relate the Word of Christ to the needs of the congregation. He must be true; he must be clear; he must be dedicated; he must himself be deep; and he must be relevant. He must undertake his work with a determination to bring all those whom he contacts into a closer relationship with God. His constant fight is to keep the minds of his congregation centered on the spiritual rather than the material. He must lead them to "seek first the Kingdom of God" and then they will "look not at the things which are seen, but at the things which are not seen; for the things which are seen are temporal, but the things which are not seen are eternal" (2 Corinthians 4:18).

Even though he uses the tools of the public speaker to make

his work more effective, his aim is higher. George Sweazey has expressed it well:

> A sermon is not a public speech, it is an element in a worshipping experience. Preaching may be studied by itself, just as hymnology or the sacraments may be considered separately, but it must always be remembered that the sermon is just one part of an extended experience with God. From this it gets a power that, as a lecture, it could never have. All the deep human needs that make worship necessary make preaching necessary because the sermon is one of the most powerful means for bringing about the encounter between God and men.[6]

ASSIGNMENT

The Role of the Preacher

Write a paper (essay) of about 1,000 words which incorporates ideas you have taken from several sources but which draws your own conclusions on some but not necessarily all of the following, as the teacher assigns:

a. What is preaching?
b. The value of homiletics
c. The function of the preacher in today's church
d. The outcomes to expect from sermons

Write in third person and use well an acceptable style of footnotes and bibliography.

As the teacher assigns, the essay can address the above topics directly or may approach them indirectly by including them as you write on any of the following themes:

---

[6]George E. Sweazey, *Preaching the Good News* (Englewood Cliffs, N.J.: Prentice Hall, 1976), 4.

a. My Personal Goals as a Preacher (may be done in first person if desired)
b. A Preacher I Consider To Be Effective (either a biblical or a modern-day preacher)
c. A Congregation and Its Minister
d. An Effective Sermon I Have Heard
e. Preparing to Preach

The Personal Qualities Of the Preacher

2

"Be thou an ensample" — 1 Timothy 4:12

INTRODUCTION

There may be differences of opinion regarding many facets of the preacher's life and work, but on one matter there is total agreement: *a good preacher must be a good man.* Much of the power of Jesus' spoken word came from the power of its source—a sinless life. Paul, John, Peter, Stephen—all, likewise, added force to their words by the devotion of their lives.

In Chapter 1, *the role of the preacher was described as one of leading his congregation to a deeper spirituality, and thus helping each one he touches to reach heaven.* He seeks to develop devotion to the spirit coupled with a flight from the flesh. The preacher must lead his hearers to "abhor that which is evil; cleave to that which is good" (Romans 12:9).

If this is the minister's goal, *he will find no greater weapon in his arsenal than his own good character.* Too often the preacher and his family *feel sorry* for themselves; they indulge

27

in "self-pity," bemoaning the care they must take to avoid criticism. Rather than bewailing scrutiny of his own life, the preacher should delight that he has this additional opportunity for achieving his goal. Paul urged Timothy to use his personal character to advantage: "Be thou an ensample to them that believe, in word, in manner of life, in love, in faith, in purity" (1 Timothy 4:12, ASV).

From ancient rhetoricians to the modern, *ethical proof* (a means of invention) has been given a place of importance in the accomplishment of persuasion. Aristotle said: "*The character* [ἦθος] *of the speaker* is a cause of persuasion when the speech is so uttered as to make him worthy of belief." In fact, he continues, "We might affirm that *his character* [ἦθος] is the most potent of all the means to persuasion."[1] Quintilian, the famous classical rhetorician from the first century A.D., adds his testimony: "My aim, then, is the education of the perfect orator. The first essential for such an one is that he should *be a good man*, and consequently we demand of him not merely the possession of exceptional gifts of speech, but of *all the excellences of character as well.*"[2] Taking its place along with *logical* and *emotional* appeal, ethical appeal may be defined as *the appeal of the speaker's personality*. Interpreted broadly, it involves the speaker's personal qualities and reputation, his experiences, his "common touch" with the audience, and most of all, the way he utilizes these in the message itself. Rhetoricians, then, have long recognized that a speaker's character is of equal value with his logical and emotional appeals.

The relationship of a man's life and his message is easily seen. When the minister urges faith during difficult times, his own exemplary conduct at his father's death will lend force to his sermon. When he argues for high moral standards, his own pure and happy life will strengthen his contention. When he asks for sacrifice, his own cheerful liberality will set the proper tone for his request. When he pleads for teachers to plan their

---

[1]Aristotle, *The Rhetoric of Aristotle*, Translated by Lane Cooper (New York: Appleton-Century-Crofts, 1932), 8, 9, I.2.1.

[2]Quintilian, *The Institutio Oratoria*, Translated by H. H. Butler. 4 vols. (Cambridge, MA: Harvard University Press, 1921-22), 9, 11.

lessons carefully, his own careful study habits will reinforce his plea.

In addition to the *ethical appeal* through which the preacher's good character strengthens his sermons, his good qualities also set the right *example* for the congregation. Thus he both urges and exemplifies Christian conduct. Jesus had these two in mind when he said, *"But whosoever shall do and teach them, he shall be called great in the kingdom of heaven"* (Matthew 5:19). Paul urged Timothy, likewise, *"Take heed to thyself and to thy teaching"* (1 Timothy 4:16). Is it significant that in both cases example is put before teaching?

While it should not be the main consideration, a preacher and his family must, of course, recognize the *harm* their personal lives can do to the cause which they serve. Truth becomes void of influence when it comes out of hypocrisy. Paul stresses this very point in Romans 2:21, 22: "You who teach others, will you not teach yourself? While you preach against stealing, do you steal? You who say that one must not commit adultery, do you commit adultery?" The minister, then, who contradicts his preaching with his life, will void both.

One of the certainties of preaching, then, is that no minister can serve effectively if his conduct is out of harmony with his message. On the other hand, no preacher can reach his maximum potential without the benefit of ethical appeal.

Discussion Question: Who are some preachers who have either strengthened or weakened their proclamation by their personal lives?

Just what are those personal qualities which a preacher must have to be an effective spokesman for God, a trainer of souls? Of the countless words which have been used to describe various traits of character, it is difficult to fix on a reasonable number which sum up the kind of person the preacher ought to be. There are, however, ten qualities which, when interpreted broadly, may be used to include the most basic and vital personal qualities for a minister of the Word.

TEN PERSONAL QUALITIES
(1) A SENSE OF BURDEN. Preaching is difficult, con-

suming work. Its material rewards are not as great as those offered in many other occupations while its problems and demands are often much greater. A preacher *has little privacy himself* but is asked to share the most private griefs, fears, and pains of others. He is on constant call to engage in those experiences which drain him physically, mentally and emotionally. *Only one reward can truly make preaching worth what it takes from a man: the spiritual satisfaction of carrying a small burden for Him who carried a great burden for us.*

The preacher who does not feel the "burden of the Lord" cannot receive the thrill of bearing it and cannot long, therefore, feel that the assets in preaching outweigh the liabilities. This burden includes a recognition of (1) the length of eternity, (2) the guilt of sinfulness, (3) the value of souls, and (4) a depth of commitment.[3] This sense of burden is very closely related to "the call to preach."

There are certain preachers who seem to stand clearly apart from others as messengers for God. They grip the audience and establish a directness others do not reach. This is often due to the deep sense of burden that causes an audience to sense the preacher's closeness to God. This *closeness to God becomes a magnet which draws preacher and listener together.*

(2) SINCERITY. One of the most basic of all traits for a preacher is sincerity. Nothing will deafen a congregation more quickly than for them to regard the preacher as a hypocrite; and nothing, on the other hand, will make an audience more receptive or more willing to overlook shortcomings than a deep conviction and earnestness on the part of the speaker. Writers in homiletics have used a host of terms to describe this quality: moral earnestness, personal piety, unselfish devotion, zeal to serve.

Such sincerity grows from a concern for the lost; it blossoms into diligent work; its fruit will be the joy of bringing a soul to the throne of God. Paul charged Timothy to serve with "love out of a pure heart and a good conscience and faith unfeigned"

---

[3]See Ian McPherson, *The Burden of the Lord* (Nashville: Abingdon Press, 1955), 10-12.

(1 Timothy 1:5). Jesus spoke of "purity of heart" and of "singleness of heart" or oneness of purpose.

Sincerity, then, is basic to a preacher's effectiveness, and without it he has little chance of success. This quality begins with the *obsession to preach*, expands to fill one's life with *an awareness of the all-importance of the spiritual*, and ends when the preacher can say with Paul, "I have fought a good fight, I have kept the faith, I have finished my course" (2 Timothy 4:7).

(3) ENTHUSIASM. Related to and growing from sincerity is the quality of enthusiasm. Jesus spoke of those who "hunger and thirst after righteousness," and Paul exhibited this quality when he declared the Word "with tears . . . both publicly and from house to house" (Acts 20:19, 20). It is enthusiasm that breeds the *courage to speak one's convictions* even though his job or his life is at stake. John the Baptist showed such enthusiastic determination when he told Herod he had no right to his brother's wife.

With enthusiasm also comes *optimism* and a preacher must be optimistic. He must not lose his spark when others are ready to quit; he must not flee from dark clouds but look for the light. In many situations it is the preacher who must revive sinking spirits or else there will be no one to stem the tide of defeat.

The kind of enthusiasm meant here is not an effervescence which bubbles from the surface with nothing underneath. Nor should the preacher become so unrealistic in his optimism that his sincerity is questioned. Rather this enthusiasm may be equated with a firm conviction that, by the power of God, one has the "faith which overcomes the world."

Discussion Questions: How does a preacher keep his enthusiasm high? Does a preacher have to speak rapidly with loud volume to be an enthusiastic preacher?

(4) HUMILITY. The first beatitude declares, "Blessed are the poor in spirit, for theirs is the kingdom of heaven" (Matthew 5:3). Poverty of spirit means the *knowledge of one's own limitations and a recognition that "it is not in man that walketh to direct his steps"* (Jeremiah 10:23). Every church member knows what some preachers do not: The publican in Jesus' story would make a much better preacher than the Pharisee. There is

a tendency for the world to exalt a preacher, and unfortunately, there is a tendency for preachers to accept it.

A preacher is often called a "minister" and as such he must minister to the needs of people. No preacher whose eyes are turned always on himself, however, can be sensitive to the needs of others. This humility is seen when the preacher takes whatever time it requires to talk with the most uneducated member of his congregation about some spiritual problem. It is seen in his willingness to work side by side with the members in a special project at the church building or in distributing handbills. Most of all, the preacher's humility is put to the test when he has the *opportunity to do some good act which no one will know about and for which he will receive no praise from men.*

Too many preachers *require constant praise as a fuel for their enthusiasm.* They are unwilling to perform any tasks which will not gain for them approving words and handshakes. The joy they feel when learning of the success of another preacher is tinged with an uneasy sorrow and envy.

Humility is one of the most difficult qualities for the preacher to acquire and keep. He is, usually, above the level of the congregation in intelligence, training, and zeal for God. It is easy for him to think of himself as better than others because he knows more about the Scriptures, has a deeper insight into the work of the church, and actually does more visiting and teaching than other members. It is an easy step from a recognition of this to an inordinate pride in his own accomplishments. A preacher must keep before himself constantly the fact that, if his ability is greater than another's, he should thank God, not condemn his brother; if, because of greater opportunity, he has excelled another, he should humble himself before the Lord, not exalt himself before the church. What does anyone have which he does not owe to his parents, his teachers, his family, his friends, and his God? A recognition of this dependence will help one to a greater poverty of spirit.

Genuine humility is closely akin to unselfishness—putting oneself out of the picture in order to look at others. Paul's description of the aspects of love in 1 Corinthians can also be taken as a picture of humility: patience; kindness; not envious; not boastful, arrogant, or rude; seeks not its own; is not provoked. *A preacher, then, must put aside self to seek God, the kingdom, and others.* Paul expressed the ultimate degree of such humility and unselfishness when he told the Romans (9:3) that he could wish himself "anathema from Christ" if it would mean the salvation of others.

(5) MEEKNESS. Another foundation stone in the minister's character must be the quality of meekness, perhaps the most frequently misunderstood quality in the teaching of Jesus. Meekness is often mistaken for weakness, and many who lack courage, stamina and strength are called meek.

Numbers 12:3 speaks of Moses as being meek "above all the men that were upon the face of the earth." But why? Was Moses cowardly? Far from it. He is called meek because he could "take it." When the Israelites murmured and complained against him, he was patient and did not become personally affronted.

Meekness, then, is that quality of being difficult to insult. Sometimes this quality is called being "thick-skinned," and the opposite of meekness is called "wearing your feelings on your sleeve" or having "a chip on your shoulder." A preacher must combine the *hide of an alligator with the gentleness of a dove.* He must be sensitive to the needs of those with whom he works, while at the same time insensitive to the barbs which will be thrown at him and his family. Meekness is the response of humility to attack.

Meekness includes a generous portion of tact—the ability to say the right things and to refrain from saying the wrong things. Another component of meekness is the quality of being a *peacemaker.* The preacher must not only be "easy to get along with" himself, but must have this quality to a contagious degree. He not only mends breaks after they occur, but as a lightning rod sweeps electricity from clouds to keep the charge from building to higher levels, so the preacher must discharge ill will before it builds to hate with its subsequent devastation. Just as the preacher is the object of much praise, he is also the target of much criticism. When such occasions arise, as they certainly will, he must conduct himself as Moses, Stephen,

Paul, and Jesus did: not retaliating in sarcasm, gossip, or slander, nor splitting the church while attempting to justify himself; rather he must return good for evil, pray for those who despitefully use him and love his enemies. Many charges are better left unanswered and those who rush to print a vindication of themselves usually add more heat with little light.

(6) PATIENCE. Like a well-cut diamond held in the light, patience has many facets: *determination, dependability, long-suffering, steadfastness, endurance, fortitude, perseverance, self-control*. A preacher's goals, for the most part, are long-range aims which take years to achieve, and even then his work is not finished. When he has done his best and seems to have made progress, there remains so much to do. On other occasions, the preacher feels he has done his best and has nothing to show for his efforts. Yet he must not give up in discouragement.

In the life of every preacher there will be moments when he feels that his work is in vain, when he has done his best only to fail, when he feels completely inadequate to the task. The young man to whom the preacher has given hours of training will fall into bad company and become involved in stealing; the family whom he seems to be pulling together will suddenly explode; the prospect whom he has visited and taught and who has promised to accept Christ will suddenly grow cold; and the weak member who seemed to be starting to grow will wither and die. The church with whom he has labored and for whom he has lit and tended the fire will grow dim as though the light would fail completely.

In such moments as these the preacher must recall that after Jesus spent three years with Judas, His own apostle betrayed Him with a hypocritical touch of the lips. Some of the Jews who on Sunday cried out, "Hosanna," on Friday screamed, "Crucify Him." Mark was a disappointment to Paul, and Demas forsook him completely. These illustrations merely underscore the words of Paul in 1 Corinthians 3:6, "I planted, Apollos watered; but God gave the increase." The preacher's work is to plant and water and "each shall receive his own reward according to his own labor" (1 Corinthians 3:8). Too often ministers tend to measure their work in *human* rather than *divine* terms. In God's record book a man is rewarded for the sincerity and diligence of his work, not in the number of additions or the amount of the contribution. The "increase" is God's part. A preacher should neither be overly discouraged when the increase fails to come or overly exalted when it does.

A preacher, then, must labor with all his might, but, at the same time, remember that his strength cometh from the Lord. He must "not grow weary in well doing, for in due season we shall reap if we faint not" (Galatians 6:9).

(7) PURITY. Although implied in other traits, purity demands special mention as important to preachers. In addition to being under special observation, *the preacher is also under special temptation.*

The preacher must observe *unusual precaution* to be certain that no moral charge can be laid against him—whether true or false. He should not, ordinarily, for example, visit in the home of a woman who is alone without his wife or another man with him. If he is in the church building alone, he should leave his office door open when a woman comes to see him. The preacher, too, should be careful with his physical contacts, not in any way appearing to be "too familiar."

The preacher should stand for high moral standards and should live and think consistently with what he preaches. The literature he reads and pictures he sees should be the kind he recommends from the pulpit.

If these suggestions seem extreme, one needs only to recall the many effective preachers whose work has been ruined and the congregations which have been torn apart because of either immoral deeds or charges of such against the preacher.

Discussion Question: What are some of the special temptations by which Satan will attack a preacher's purity?

(8) INTELLECTUAL COMPETENCE. Anyone must bring to his work certain basic equipment. The high jumper must have strong legs, the violinist must have nimble fingers, a stevedore must have strong arms, and the lifeguard must have good eyes. Since a preacher's work is largely mental, he must have a ready grasp of ideas and a long retention of them, but no preacher can achieve a very great degree of success who does not like to

study. As indicated in Chapter 1, the preacher's role is primarily one of leading his congregation to a deeper spirituality. The depth to which he can lead others is largely dependent upon his own spiritual depth—a depth which will be in direct ratio to his personal study and devotion in the Scriptures.

Paul urged Timothy to "give heed to reading" (1 Timothy 4:13), and told him "Give diligence to show thyself approved unto God, a workman that needeth not to be ashamed, handling aright the word of truth" (2 Timothy 2:15).

Quintilian concluded that *the perfect orator would have to know everything*, and the same is true of the perfect preacher. Jesus, indeed, was the perfect preacher because He knew everything, even the thoughts of men. There is nothing a preacher can know which cannot be made of value to him: history, literature, science, art, agriculture, politics, psychology, medicine, business, sociology, advertising, philosophy, music, sports, current events, foreign language, astronomy. The broader his knowledge, the greater the force and variety in his power of illustration and application.

The preacher's mental capacity must contain a rich imagination, a generous endowment of originality, a power of vivid illustration, and an insatiable thirst for truth.

The best preachers have *active imaginations and a touch of the artist in them.* A flair for an exciting expression or thrilling story is as important in good preaching as the capacity for logical arrangement.

In sum, a preacher must not only be above average in mental capacity, but must have a special turn of mind toward intellectual pursuits. His mind is his basic tool, and it must be clothed with a broad knowledge and specially fitted with a perceptive understanding of the Word of God.

(9) GOOD HEALTH. Although a preacher's mind is his principal tool, this mind is encased in a body and is affected by the state of that body. The physical demands upon the preacher are great. His work is strenuous by any standards—long hours, constant pressure, emotional strain. Like the doctor, the physician of the soul is on twenty-four hour call, and his work is exhausting.

From this it is obvious that the preacher must have good health or else he will be unable to continue long under the rigors of the work. There is another implication, though. No person who is physically fatigued is able to have a cheerful disposition or think clearly—essentials for the preacher.

Since his effectiveness as a minister of the Word is directly related to his health, the preacher needs to take care of his body. While he should work hard, he should also arrange for rest. He needs a set day, or two half-days a week for recreation and freedom from responsibilities. For most men this is a necessity for maintaining physical and mental well-being. If a minister shows himself a hard worker at other times, no one will object to his taking some time each week for recreation.

Unfortunately, moderation in this regard is difficult to find. So many preachers seem either to refuse to take a moment for rest and recreation or to make half their appointments for the "no. 1 tee."

(10) LEADERSHIP. A preacher *must* be a leader. The Bible does not call him "the pastor" of a flock, nor is he a dictator or administrative head, but he is, nonetheless, a leader. He sounds a call for action; he assists in planning; he urges a response; he not only points the way but shows it. *He must be aggressive, zealous, determined, idealistic, well-organized, diligent, and informed—all qualities of leadership.* Effectiveness in both written and oral communication are also qualities of leadership which the preacher needs. While the Scriptures call for the preacher to exert his leadership under the oversight of elders, certain qualities of leadership are essential to the accomplishment of his task. No one to whom people do not react positively can lead them to "higher ground" spiritually.

SUMMARY

These ten qualities, taken together, paint a clear picture of the man who is qualified to preach. While no person can have all these traits to perfection, one who is obviously weak in any one of them or who appears to lack the capacity for developing them should recognize this inadequacy, and, if it is too great, he should seek to serve the Lord in some other way than as a preacher. Those who have the basic ingredients should turn their energies to a continual development of these qualities—a constant growth toward Christlike perfection. Although this goal is impossible to attain, the effort spent in attempting to do so will bring dividends into the preacher's life.

What if a man is *called to preach* who is obviously lacking in these qualities? What if a man has the qualities but is not called? Great discussion has arisen about the "call to preach." Some have believed that a supernatural call is required, while others have said there is no call at all. Although the purpose here is not to discuss in full the question of the miraculous in the twentieth century, the trend today is correctly away from the belief that a man must experience a supernatural "vision" as a "call" *to preach*. One is called to preach, nonetheless. Nathaniel Burton summed up the natural elements in the call to preach as the "gift," a "certain convergence of the man's circumstances toward the work ministerial," and "the united advice of judicious friends."[4] Batsell Barrett Baxter concludes, "A man may assume that he is 'called to preach' when his natural qualifications are such as are needed by the minister, when he feels certain that God desires him as a public proclaimer of the gospel, and when he himself desires to preach to such a degree that he could never be quite conscience-free should he decline the opportunity to preach."[5]

Paul expressed the burden which must be felt by every worthy minister of the gospel: "Woe unto me, if I preach not the gospel" (1 Corinthians 9:16). And to the Romans (1:14-15) he wrote: "I am debtor both to the Greeks and to Barbarians, both to the wise and to the foolish. So, as much as in me is, I am ready to preach the gospel to you also that are in Rome."

Discussion Question: Do you feel the call to preach?

---

[4]Batsell Barrett Baxter, *The Heart of the Yale Lectures* (New York: Macmillan Co., 1947), 6, 7; quoted from Nathaniel J. Burton, *In Pulpit and Parish* (New York: Macmillan Co., 1925), 36-39.

[5]Ibid., 12, 13.

ASSIGNMENT

The Personal Qualities of the Preacher

Write one paragraph on each of the questions below. You may use references and/or state your own opinions.

1. Why is the preacher's personal character of importance in his mission?
2. List and describe the three personal qualities you believe most essential for the preacher.
3. What two personal traits are particularly undesirable for a preacher?
4. Is a man called to preach?

3 | The Process of Preparation

"Give diligence to present thyself approved unto God, a workman that needeth not to be ashamed" — 2 Timothy 2:15

INTRODUCTION

When Jesus sent out the twelve with the "limited commission," He instructed, "Be not anxious how or what ye shall speak: for it shall be given you in that hour what ye shall speak" (Matthew 10:19). In the miraculous age of prophecy, tongues, interpretations, and knowledge, this was excellent instruction for preachers and produced extremely effective proclamation. But the preacher of today who steps into the pulpit without preparation, though he needs one, neither deserves nor receives a miracle.

What, then, can and should the preacher do before he rises to relay the message of God to the people? If God does not give him the message directly, how does it come and what must the preacher do to facilitate a good response? Some, at first thought, might suggest that all he must do is to read and explain some Bible verse. Further consideration, however, would disclose that

41

not all passages lend themselves to such use and that "explanation" can vary from random clichés to linguistic exegesis.

The conclusion, then, is inescapable: the present messenger of God must select a particular spiritual message suited to the needs of the audience, find materials to clarify and emphasize the message, determine an order and arrangement, employ words which best express the thought, and speak with clarity and force. *This process of speech preparation, particularly as applied to the sermon, is the subject of the remainder of this book. In this chapter we view the process as a whole, and in later chapters, observe it piece by piece.*

THE CREATIVE SPARK

Almost every sermon worth thirty minutes of the listener's time begins with a creative spark—that instantaneous insight when a man says, "That's the lesson they need." This "seed-thought"[1] frequently comes while reading and meditating on the Scriptures or while reading some other book.[2] The flash may come, however, while listening to a sermon or lecture, while reviewing notebooks or files or previous "jottings," while watching television or a movie, while conversing, while fishing, while driving, or while dreaming. While the sparks seem spontaneous, actually they result from striking a carefully tempered mind against the flint of Scripture, human experience, or spiritual need (Chapters 4 and 5).

As any Boy Scout can testify, however, many sparks fly from the flint and steel which are not caught in the tinder, and are, therefore, lost as quickly as they came. For this reason every preacher should have always at hand a pen and paper on which to catch these flashes. While one word may be sufficient to recall the thought, it is preferable to jot down as much as possible.[3] Whether the preacher uses index cards, a pocket-

---

[1]Andrew W. Blackwood, *The Preparation of Sermons* (Nashville: Abingdon-Cokesbury Press, 1948), 37.

[2]See Ilian T. Jones, *Principles and Practice of Preaching* (Nashville: Abingdon Press, 1956), 69-73.

[3]See Webb B. Garrison, *Creative Imagination in Preaching* (Nashville: Abingdon Press, 1960), 52-61.

sized notebook, or odd scraps of papers is not the important thing. What is important is that he capture the spark and preserve its life until it can ignite love, zeal, or understanding in an entire congregation.

Of course, a systematic method is better than a haphazard one, and a plan for recording, retaining, and reviewing these "eternal glimpses" is fundamental. Some experienced preachers use a file folder for ideas in certain general areas such as "Holy Spirit," "Love," "Repentance," and "Visitation." Others utilize a card file in which to deposit ideas or illustrations which should be preserved for later reference. While it is important to "plan the work," it is even more important to "work the plan." (See Appendix for more suggestions on a filing system.)

From spark to leaping, spreading fire is not only the process of sermon preparation and delivery, it is also the thrill of preaching, the creative excitement. Webb Garrison calls it the "joy from discovery," and describes it as the "pleasure" which transforms "labor into a kind of recreation." "For us in the ministry," he continues, "one of the most sublime sources of pleasure is that of hearing a message from God. Along with insight into fresh truth, or a new aspect of old truth, there is likely to come joy that approaches ecstasy."[4]

This principle explains why an audience can usually tell whether the sermon is from the preacher's recent, active thinking or is an undigested regurgitation from a book of outlines or a hasty revival from his own ancient notes. If the sermon starts with the spark, it can strike fire; if it is merely the choosing of a subject, it is likely to "strike out."

SMOLDERING AND MORE FUEL

A good sermon needs smoldering time—long enough to let the spark spread in the tinder, but not so long that it dies. Blackwood labels this period "unconscious incubation,"[5] the time most ideas require to mature. The preacher who allows smoldering time between spark and flame will be amazed at the

[4]Ibid., 17.
[5]Blackwood, 39.

great amount of material he will gather by accident, and, of course, he will have greater time for study, prayer, discussion, and analysis of the theme.

"*Relaxed attention* has the strange effect of fostering discovery of things overlooked in concentration."[6] Reminiscent of Jesus' encounter with the barren fig tree, the sermon delivered before it is fully developed may have beautiful foliage, but is not likely to bear much fruit. A stillborn infant is the probable result of delivery before the end of pregnancy.

The smoldering period is the time for investigation, exegesis, analysis, research meditation, and prayer. It not only sees more material gathered than can be used in the half-hour delivery (Chapter 7), but allows the selection of the most significant pattern for organization (Chapter 6). This period also sees the selection of various key words and phrases to be used in delivery (Chapter 8).

The end result of this period is the *sermon outline*—a device for stating, in brief form, the major ideas in the sermon with their accompanying material, and in a manner which shows the exact relationship of each item to all the others. Making an outline, undoubtedly, is the finest method for pulling together the various ideas the preacher has found on a theme into a unified whole. To make a fire burn properly, the sticks must be properly arranged, not scattered loosely about.

It is important here to distinguish between the "sermon outline" and "speaker's notes." What the speaker uses in the pulpit to remind himself of what he wishes to say may range from nothing to a complete manuscript. The sermon outline, however, is that group of statements and material that constitute the theme of the sermon and its development. A preacher may, of course, use a copy of the outline he has developed as his notes, or he may take with him only a few key points or he may write out all of what he will say. The "outline" and the "notes," however, need to be clearly distinguished.

Discussion Questions: Based on your observation, how many notes should a preacher take into the pulpit with him? Should he

---

[6]Garrison, 49.

take his full outline?

Chapter 6 deals in detail with sermon organization, but since sermons will be prepared for class delivery before a study of Chapter 6, a sample outline is contained at the end of this chapter for brief study. Full sentence outlines with proper subdivisions and a careful understanding of the significance of each element on the outline should become second nature with every preacher.

THE FLAME

When the preacher steps to the pulpit, he should be on fire, burning inside with his message. It started with a spark which creatively put together a biblical truth with a human need, smoldered through a period of gathering and arranging fuel, and now bursts into flame.

He has practiced the sermon to polish his delivery; he has memorized the outline so he may give his major attention to the audience; and he has spent his last moments before entering the pulpit in quiet, intensive prayer for God to send "fire" from heaven.[7] Now he is ready to let the flame in his heart be the fuel to set the congregation afire for the Lord.

ASSIGNMENT

The Process of Preparation

Prepare a ten-minute sermon for class delivery. This sermon should have a complete outline, as shown on pages 48-51. The outline *must* conform to this pattern. You can use your own method after the course is over, but you must master this one during the course. The teacher and student should review the student's proposed outline a few days before the sermon is to be delivered in class so that problems with the plan may be dealt with before the outline is completed. Particular attention in grading this sermon will be given to using correct outline form,

---

[7]Gerald Kennedy, *His Word Through Preaching* (New York: Harper & Brother Publishers, 1947), 8.

to having a useful message, and to having a clear and forceful delivery. The technical plot, however, is not necessary for this assignment. The outline must be given to the teacher before the sermon can be delivered so he can follow the outline and make notes on it as the sermon is delivered. The material before and after the solid lines is not part of the speech as delivered but is essential for a complete outline. This sermon should be video-taped for review by the teacher and student.

Note the following outlining techniques demonstrated in the outline on pages 48-51:

1. A sermon outline begins with a title which should serve as both a means of attracting interest for the sermon when published in advance and for filing or recording the details of when and where the sermon was delivered. The title should be brief and strong, and may use curiosity or a relationship to those topics which will interest a potential listener.

2. A statement of purpose should identify a sermon as to its general type: to inform, to convince, to inspire, or to actuate (see Chapter 5). The purpose statement's second function is to identify the general content or subject matter regarding which the preacher will inform, convince, inspire, or actuate. A third and very important element of the purpose statement is to state the outcome the preacher hopes to obtain through the sermon. This portion will typically begin with the words "so that the audience will. . . . " If particular groups of the audience are to have different responses, they should be named in particular.

3. In the introduction (discussed in detail in Chapter 6) the preacher will seek to build good will with the audience, give them any necessary background information, and gain their attention to the subject. It will help the main points of the body of the sermon to stand out more clearly if the points of the introduction (and later the conclusion) begin with A, B, C, rather than I, II, III.

4. The subject sentence plays a very vital role in the outline (see Chapter 6). This is the key statement of the sermon and thus becomes the proposition or thesis around which everything else is constructed. The main points of the body are subdivisions or points of support for the subject sentence. It should be a short,

striking, memorable, complete sentence that captures the essence of the message.

5. The body of the sermon contains the main headings and their support. The main headings should all come from the same basis of division (see Chapter 6) and must be parallel in thought and in wording. Each should be a complete sentence. Developing the subject sentence with its corresponding main headings is the key element in good sermon organization. These constitute the skeleton of the sermon and should be concise, striking statements the audience can quickly grasp and identify as keys to the lesson. Each main point should be preceded by a Roman numeral to set it clearly apart. Each main heading will have several subpoints, preceded by A, B, C's, and each of these may be further subdivided with 1, 2, 3's.

The preacher will think more clearly in the outlining process if he will follow these two procedures: (1) make every point on the outline a complete sentence (although sometimes a point and its subdivisions may together make the sentence) and (2) whenever subpoints are developed there should be at least two. Where there seems to be only one, the preacher should incorporate the one subpoint into the heading to which it is related. So—no A's without a corresponding B or 1's without a corresponding 2.

6. The conclusion rounds out the sermon by a summation and an appeal for the congregation to use the sermon as indicated in the "so that" of the purpose statement (see Chapter 6). As in the introduction, start these points with A, B, C.

7. Where references have been used to develop the sermon that would be helpful to consult again if the subject were being re-studied or if questions were raised about the content, put such sources in the section for references. It is not necessary to list the Bible or a concordance in the reference section.

THE BIBLE ON MARRIAGE

Purpose: To inform the congregation about the Bible's teaching of marriage so that marriages can be stronger and children can grow up to develop homes as God would have them to be.

Introduction:

Relevance to gain attention }

    A. Look at the morning newspaper: "Estranged Husband Murders Wife," "Juvenile Delinquency Rate Shows Rapid Rise," and in the advice column, "Unhappy Wife Asks If Divorce Is the Answer." We are painfully aware of the problems in marriages today.

Facts to gain good will }

    B. But there are a vast number of happy marriages today—marriages that are a blessing to the husband and wife, to the children, and to all who come in contact with those in such families.

Appeals to affections and convictions to gain attention }

    C. A book written centuries ago can help us have such homes. It is a book from the mind of God, who made both human beings and marriage for them.

Narration to gain attention and give background }

    D. The story of the marriage of Paul and Mary shows us what happiness God intended us to find in marriage.

Subject Sentence: God's plan for marriage should be the guide for your marriage.

Subject based analysis }

Body:

    I. Marriage Is Sacred.

        A. Marriage was started by God—Genesis 2.

Quotation and explanation to clarify }

        B. Each marriage made according to His teaching is recognized by Him—Mark 10:9.

Explanation to interest and clarify }

C. Since God started marriage and is the one who joins two in marriage, He has the right to set the laws of marriage.

II. Marriage Is Honorable.

Quotation to clarify }

A. Hebrews 13:4—"Let marriage be held in honor by all men."

Quotation and explanation to clarify }

B. Paul suggests celibacy for some in 1 Corinthians 7:7, but does not command it for any.

Quotation to clarify }

C. Jesus, likewise, mentions that some may wish to remain unmarried, but does not require it of anyone—Matthew 19:10-12.

III. Marriage Is Permanent.

Quotation and explanation to clarify }

A. From Genesis 2, Mark 10, Luke 16:18, Romans 7, and 1 Corinthians 7, we learn that the Lord intended that the marriage relationship be as permanent as the two lives which agree to become one and that the ideal plan is for death only to break the bond. Sam and Mary realized this and found an answer to their problems without breaking up their marriage.

Quotation and explanation to clarify }

B. Matthew's account implies that fornication may break the relationship if the innocent party so desires and that the innocent party may remarry—Matthew 5:31; 19:2.

Quotation to clarify }

C. Separation is discouraged, but may be necessary under certain conditions—1 Corinthians 7:10f.—but even in such a case, there is a question about remarriage.

Narration to interest and motivate }

D. The story of Jan and Jolen shows the great benefit of recognizing that marriage should be permanent.

IV. Marriage Is Close.

A. The expression "one flesh" is used to describe marriage in Genesis 2:23, 24; and this means that marriage is the closest of earthly ties with the two streams of life being blended into one, being united in purpose and plan. Joe and Lou illustrate this closeness.

Quotation to clarify
Example to clarify }

B. Each is to love and respect the other: Ephesians 5:25; 1 Peter 3:7; Titus 2:4. Sue and Bob illustrate how this works.

Quotation to clarify }

C. Since marriage is so close, widows are instructed to marry "only in the Lord"—1 Corinthians 7:9—and others are much better off to do the same.

Quotation to clarify }

1. Ask those who have lived for years with a mate who is not a Christian and they will be the first to agree.

Example to convince }

2. When two who love each other can also share their love for God, they are drawn much closer to each other; but when two cannot share their spiritual life, they often have a problem which creates a growing wedge between them.

Explanation to clarify }

D. Listen to the case of the Smiths.

Narration to interest and motivate }

V. Marriage Is Purposeful.

A. In 1 Corinthians 7, Paul makes it clear that companionship is one of the purposes of marriage and one aspect of the companionship is that marriage provides the God-given relationship in which sexual desires may be righteously fulfilled.

Quotation to clarify }

B. A second purpose for marriage is the continuance of the race in bearing and training children.

Explanation to clarify }

Example to interest }
C. So use your marriage for God by making your home a radiating center for the gospel, a light to all those around, for, as important as the home is, one's relationship to God is even more important.

D. Ken and Mary illustrate how to do this.

Conclusion:

Comparison to interest }
A. Paul paid marriage a high tribute when he likened the husband/wife relationship to that between Christ and the church—Ephesians 5.

Summary }
B. Marriage was instituted by God, approved by Christ, and is regulated by the Holy Spirit.

Description to appeal }
C. If you are not yet married, then purpose to select your mate in full recognition of God's laws and purposes for marriage, making your goal to build a home in which God Himself would feel welcome.

Explanation }
D. If you already have a husband or wife, determine to work hard to improve your home; be a better husband, a better wife, a better Christian, working harder to make your home pleasing to God.

References

Baird, James O. *And I Say Unto You.* Oklahoma City: B & B Book House, 1981.

Bales, James. *Not Under Bondage.* Searcy, AR: By the Author, 1979.

Brecheen, Carl, and Paul Faulkner. *What Every Family Needs.* Austin: Journey Books, 1974.

Mayhall, Jack and Carole. *Marriage Takes More Than Love.* Colorado Springs: Navpress, 1978.

Meredith, Maurice, and Alvah Hovey. *The Divorce Question and the*

Scriptural Law of Divorce. Rosemead, CA: Old Paths Book Club, n.d.

Scott, Harvey. *Bible Study Guidance*. Oklahoma City: Telegram Book Co., 1960.

Warren, Thomas B., ed. *Your Marriage Can Be Great*. Jonesboro, AR: National Christian Press, 1978.

4 | Preaching To Needs

"Put the brethren in mind of these things"
— 1 Timothy 4:6

INTRODUCTION

How foolish it would be for the captain of a sinking ship to stand on the deck with water washing over the sides and explain to the panic-filled passengers how to excel at chess. Still more foolish, however, is it for a preacher to speak to lost souls held briefly in dying bodies only to declare to them the beauties of literature or to entertain them with his wit. A preacher is, as has often been said, a dying man speaking to dying men. How different many sermons would be if the preacher believed he were having his final opportunity to bring a lost soul to Jesus; yet, in every audience, there will likely be at least one to whom a minister will be speaking for the last time.

Such thoughts merely underscore the importance of the careful choice of subject matter for preaching. Preachers are not merely engaged in a matter of life and death, but of *heaven* or *hell*. Recognizing that, in all likelihood, he will never speak to exactly the same audience again, a preacher should take special care to strike directly at the greatest needs of his audience. How tragic it is when those who need the healing and sustaining power of the Word of God "ask" but receive no answer; "seek" and do not find; "knock" and have no opening. A preacher may deliver a homiletic masterpiece with brilliant illustrations, vivid style, incisive organization, original exegesis, and enthusiastic delivery, and yet be a miserable failure because he did not meet the needs of the congregation. Such a performance is comparable to a basketball player who displays beautiful form, perfect timing, and certain accuracy, but who shoots at the wrong goal.

The preacher must remain constantly aware that his mission is to move men toward heaven. Whatever else he may do is only incidental. No political, social, economic, or intellectual service the preacher gives can ever equal his spiritual assistance. Other needs are pressing and sometimes seem more immediate, but nothing must obscure the greatest of all needs—reconciliation with God.

FOUR KEY AIMS

A preacher will find a four-point formula very helpful as a general framework for developing his sermons. To do his work effectively, he must preach sermons that may be aptly described by four key aims each sermon should reach.

First, a sermon must be *biblical*. Unless the message is truly one from the mind of God to the people, the sermon is a failure. A sermon is biblical to the extent that it brings a message built on Scripture and accurately expresses it. The measure of being biblical, however, is not a counting of the number of Scriptures cited, for one might take his message from the secular mind and attach to it some verses. A preacher, rather, must be God's messenger, His spokesman, bringing His will to people who need it. The biblical sermon brings God's message for man's needs. Paul said, "beautiful are the feet" of preachers who bring God's "good news" (Romans 10:15).

Discussion Question: To what extent do you believe sermons today are biblical?

Second, a sermon must be *interesting*. No matter how biblical the message, it will be of no benefit if it does not gain the attention of the audience. It is easy to say that the audience should listen whether the sermon is interesting or not. Perhaps the mature Christian can be expected to follow this directive. Those most in need of the message, however, will lack that maturity. In this day when listeners are so strongly influenced by television and movies, they are entertainment oriented and tend to have short attention spans. This does not mean a sermon must be entertaining, but it does mean that it must have strong elements of interest. Particularly, the use of narration is essential to hold the attention of many in the audience.

Discussion Question: To what extent do you believe sermons today are interesting?

Third, a sermon must be *practical*. A lesson might be biblical and interesting and still not have practical application to the hearers. A sermon's practicality may deal with a moral issue that the listeners face, with coping with life's needs and problems, with practical aspects of Christianity such as how to be saved or how to worship God acceptably. Even doctrinal sermons may be practical when they help a listener know what God expects or how to teach someone else an important element in God's plan.

Much today is said about "felt needs," and preachers should help people meet those needs *they feel* with God's remedy. Yet, people sometimes have needs *they do not feel* and the preacher must help them recognize that they have such needs and then assist them in dealing with these.

Discussion Question: To what extent do you believe sermons today are practical?

Fourth, a sermon must be *significant*. A sermon might be biblical, interesting, and practical, but still not be dealing with those significant matters of life which determine eternal destiny. Of course, the practical is usually significant but the term "significant" is added to the list to keep the preacher searching for sermon topics that really do make an *eternal difference*. A sermon on mission methods, for example, might be biblical, interesting, practical, and significant to one audience, but not significant at all to one where mission work is not an immediate need. Each time a preacher thinks he has found the subject for a particular audience and occasion, he should ask, *"Is this the most significant lesson I could bring to this audience at this time?"*

Discussion Question: To what extent do you believe sermons today are significant?

BASIC AUDIENCE ANALYSIS

Having seen the basic framework of making sermons biblical, interesting, practical, and significant, the preacher must move to specific information about his audience. To meet needs, a preacher must know his congregation. In the terms of the speech theorist, he must *analyze his audience*. And the more he learns about them the better.

Exactly what should a preacher know about his audience? It is obvious, of course, that the preacher, like any speaker, must know the *size* of the audience, the *age* and *educational levels* represented, the *occasion* for their gathering, their *occupations* and *backgrounds*, their *cultural* and *economic status*, *political* and *religious affiliations, attitudes* toward his subject, and the *proportion of men and women* and their *marital status*.

In most preaching occasions, however, the audience is heterogeneous with such differing ages, educational levels, and backgrounds that generalizations are difficult. About the best a preacher can do is to become fully aware of the different *groups* represented and the proportion they make of the audience: *teenagers, farmers, union members, mothers, college graduates, businessmen, retirees, Democrats,* and *many other such groups.* By knowing the groups thus represented and the general characteristics of those in such groups, he can get some indication of the characteristics of his audience.

These standard items for audience analysis will assist the preacher in a number of ways. This information will help him in choosing and making the proper approach to his subject as he considers the needs of these groups in his audience. It will also help him to select appropriate illustrations and supporting material, and in adapting his appeal to the prior convictions of the audience.[1]

FUNDAMENTAL SPIRITUAL NEEDS

To achieve true effectiveness, however, *the minister must go far beyond such surface consideration in analyzing his audience.* He must discover the spiritual needs, the conflicts, the temptations, and the problems of those to whom he speaks.

He must look behind the smile and handshake at the door to the inner struggle going on in most of his audience. If Paul could confess the need for "buffeting his body" in order to win his personal fight, few Christians could claim to be so advanced as to have no fight to make.

But what is the nature of this conflict within and how can a preacher understand it? The problems with which the preacher is concerned grow from a *soil* with three basic ingredients: *(1) the continual struggle between the physical and the spiritual, (2) the satisfaction of inborn drives, and (3) the solution to emotional problems.* These three form the triangular foundation upon which other problems are erected, and, while the superstructure is constantly changing as some matters are solved and others forgotten, the base is constant. Before the preacher can meet the real needs of his people, he must understand the soil from which their longings and problems spring. He does not, of course, center all his sermons on these basic themes, but if he looks only at the problems which show above the ground, he will often fail to touch the real needs. The preacher must devote himself to the spiritual development of his congregation, to preparing them for heaven, and to assisting them to adjust to the present life.

THE PHYSICAL vs. THE SPIRITUAL

Much of what goes on in the minds of the congregation arises from the unending conflict between the physical and the spiritual. This topic, in fact, is perhaps the most recurring theme in

---

[1]More information on audience analysis can be found in any standard public speaking textbook.

the Bible. *Adam and Eve* were the first to face this choice and, unfortunately for all their descendants, they chose the physical. *Moses,* on the other hand, chose "rather to share ill treatment with the people of God, than to enjoy the pleasure of sin for a season" (Hebrews 11:25). Even *David,* "a man after God's own heart," found Bathsheba more appealing than his conviction to righteous principles. Throughout the time of the judges and the kings, the Israelites kept wandering away from God, whom they could not see, for idols they could see. *Judas* sold his Master for thirty pieces of silver, but *Stephen* went to his death rather than surrender what he knew was right.

The Scriptures often refer to the appeal of the physical as "*the world,*" "*the carnal,*" "*mammon,*" or "*the flesh.*" These are opposed by "*the heavenly*" and "*the spirit.*" To the Corinthians, Paul described the conflict in these terms: "Look not at the things which are seen, but at the things which are not seen: for the things which are seen are temporal; but the things which are not seen are eternal" (2 Corinthians 4:18). Peter warned his readers to "abstain from fleshly lusts which war against the soul" (1 Peter 2:11).

To live on the spiritual plane and not on the fleshly, one must develop a faith strong enough to give reality to what cannot be seen: God, Christ, the Holy Spirit, heaven, hell, love, treasures in heaven. Faith is the conviction that things "not seen" are just as real as are the "seen." It is quite easy to live on the fleshly plane, to buy the goods which the devil sells from his wide open displays: money, power, pride, earthly wisdom, passion, retaliation, "getting ahead" of others. This is the obvious, unrestrained life and takes no faith at all.

One of the ever-present needs in each member of every audience, then, is to see the spiritual realm with greater reality, to place greater importance on spiritual values, to make decisions in an eternal perspective, to give spiritual matters an ever-increasing priority while placing less and less importance on material things.

Most of a preacher's sermons should have a positive effect in building this active faith. He may tell of Abraham, who saw that spiritual city "with foundations"; of Ruth, who chose an unseen

God above the idols of her native Moab; or of Barnabas, who gave his material goods for a spiritual end. He may expound passages which tell of "treasures in heaven," being "born of the water and the spirit," "renewing of the mind," or "growing in the grace and knowledge of Jesus Christ."

He must also show materialism in its true light as the destroyer of the soul. James graphically portrays planting of the *seed* of lust, growing the *plant* of sin, and reaping the *fruit* of death. The truth of the matter, James goes on, is that Satan's way is false for "every good and perfect gift is from above" (James 1:14-17).

INBORN DRIVES

Much of man's inner turmoil and need also grow from the second of the three elements of the soil: the satisfaction of inborn drives. Like an electric current, these desires surge constantly through persons and their fulfillment is the continual objective. Each drive is divinely given and is for man's own well-being. Yet, God, who gave us all these basic drives to make our lives better, knew that a person who attempts to fulfill them all without restraint will find himself or herself mired in a quicksand of desire that will make life miserable and also harmful to others. So He has revealed to us the limits that belong on each drive to make its satisfaction sufficient for our good and yet without bringing ourselves into harm. To go beyond these God-given limits brings frustration, conflict, and sin.

The preacher renders a most important service, then, when he relates Christianity to these wants of man, for, in so doing, he makes religion both practical and spiritual. Too often preachers stress the responsibilities and sacrifices of Christianity without mentioning that the blessings received "both in this life and the life which is to come" far more than outweigh what the Christian must give up. The preacher, moreover, should emphasize the point that nothing which God has placed beyond the limits is ultimately in our own best interests. Murder, stealing, fornication, drunkenness, covetousness, lying—none of these is ultimately good for either man or society. God, then, has revealed the principles of Christianity which allow each drive to be fulfilled to a reasonable degree while the individual and society are protected. At the same time, one who observes these limits is serving his Maker and developing a Christlike character.

The Christian plan for fulfillment of the drives in every person is the best ever devised. It avoids the extremes of the Stoic who says, "Avoid pleasure," and of the hedonist who says, "Pleasure is everything." The truth is that man's drives are much like the controls on a stereo set. One often misses the best sounds by running everything—volume, treble, bass—at their highest levels. So when one tries to push every drive, or any drive, for that matter, to its complete gratification, he will find confusion and frustration.

God has given us good and beautiful ways to fulfill each drive, but He has also told us where to stop by identifying as sins those actions which lie beyond the limits. Those who accept these restraints will be much happier now and have eternal satisfaction after death.

A good way to visualize this concept is shown below:

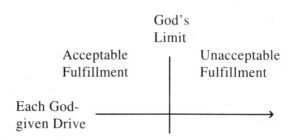

"Lust is the desire to go beyond the limit." "The flesh," "the world," "the carnal" describe those actions which are beyond the limit and are, therefore, unacceptable.

A brief examination of each drive will suggest the good fulfillment which God recommends and the sins which lie beyond God's restraints. A preacher's work, over a period of time, should bring his congregation to this understanding.

SELF-PRESERVATION. God has made man want to maintain his life and keep himself from physical harm, and that, of course, is beneficial. One must seek these ends within the bounds of honesty and temperance, however; the one who gorges himself with food under the flag of self-preservation is following the devil's plan of unrestrained lust, and is not serving his own best interest. To indulge in ego-satisfaction to the point of excessive pride is another example of carrying self-preservation too far. Self-preservation must be tempered with unselfishness or it becomes a cancer which destroys a person in uncontrolled desire. The preacher's work, then, must inculcate principles to guide this desire within proper and suitable channels.

SEX. Contrary to the belief of some, there is no evil in sex itself; only its abuses are wrong. Just as self-preservation properly leads man to care for himself, so sex provides for procreation of the race and gives something special and unifying to the husband/wife relationship. God limits the fulfillment of the sexual drive to those married to each other, however, so it will have special significance for husbands and wives and to protect society against children without a proper home. Fornication, adultery, and lasciviousness, therefore, are beyond God's limits and are sinful since they are not for man's ultimate good. When preachers provide proper teaching on this matter, they are not only strengthening God's first divine institution, the home, but are also helping the members of their congregations to avoid the paths of sinful fulfillment which lead to misery, guilt feelings, and destruction. The prophets of the "new morality," it might be added, have nothing new and certainly do not have biblical morality. With so much misunderstanding and abuse related to the sexual desire, a preacher can serve his congregation well to help them grasp and follow God's teaching on sex so they will enjoy its benefits and avoid its ills.

Discussion Question: How can the drive of sex be related to the diagram on the previous page?

SOCIAL APPROVAL. The desire for approbation makes it possible for men to band together in social living for the well-being of all. Jesus' teaching on love for neighbor, kindness, meekness, humility, peace, patience, and self-control are all designed to help the Christian receive the approval of both his fellow man and God. Christian service, likewise, will win approval from others. On the other hand, the dispositional sins of hate, malice, jealousy, and anger separate friends, while selfishness destroys marriages, business relationships, and nations. The preacher can help his congregation enjoy social approval to the proper extent while avoiding its misuse. He must especially warn against "peer pressures" which lead many into sinful pursuits.

AFFECTIONS. Related to social approval is the desire for close personal ties, "to love and to be loved." Such affections are a basic part of home and family life. God made us to want to have close ties with others and no families are as close as those in which father, mother, and children are Christian, thus following the principle of concern for others ahead of self. The love available in Christian fellowship also provides an avenue for fulfillment of this drive. On the other hand, those who are too anxious to have friends can fall into many "hurtful and foolish lusts."

POSSESSIONS. From the reach of the infant for his first toy, every person longs for possessions of his own. It is this desire which sparks most people to work harder in their secular occupations. The recent demise of communism is an indication that a system which denies this basic drive cannot meet the needs of mankind. Confined to its proper limits, the drive to possess provides a most important motivation in daily routine; but beyond its proper limits, the desire for possessions becomes insatiable and leads one into a vicious cycle of dissatisfaction. Christian principles of honesty, thrift, and stewardship are basic to a proper satisfaction of this desire; but coveting, envy, materialism, and sorrow await the one who goes beyond God's limits. In our age of materialism, God's Word can be of tremendous help in putting possessions in perspective.

POWER. Man instinctively desires to be free from restraint and most wish positions of leadership. Without this drive, a free society cannot exist, nor can initiative be found in the home, the business, the school, or the church. Jesus and Paul both spoke about freedom. Since greed and ambition spring from the unlimited desire for power, a Hitler or a Stalin plunges nations into conflict. Christianity puts the drive for power into its proper setting by combining it with humility and love.

PLEASURE. God Himself must be a lover of beauty for no artist can equal God's painting of a sunset or His forest symphony. He has given man the capacity for appreciating the beautiful and the pleasurable, and man enjoys the satisfaction of all his senses. There is, however, a constant danger that pleasure will become the controlling drive in one's life so that he lives for the lust of the flesh and not for the fruit of the Spirit. Again it is God who provides the bounds by providing examples from Eve to Demas of those who have fallen into the snare of Satan, having been lured by the "world." The preacher must help his hearers to maintain a divine perspective. Enjoyment is good and is needed for a useful life but the lust for entertainment is destructive to a person or a nation. Finding this balance in our time is especially difficult when sports and entertainment are such strong elements of our society and leisure time is more abundant than in most previous ages.

CONVICTIONS. Man needs something to believe, and as already seen, he needs boundaries for his activities. Christianity can provide these convictions. How unfortunate that some have sought to take from Christianity any doctrine which might be controversial, thus stripping it of much of its force and value. It is interesting in this connection to note that the fastest growing religions in America in recent years have been those offering the stronger, more definite doctrine to which one can anchor. Those which have offered only "relativism" have made slower growth or have declined. Preachers, like parents, need to exert positive direction for those who depend upon them, and should provide sufficient teaching to provide a sound base for solid convictions. Surely the Word of God provides the best foundation on which to build one's set of convictions.

EXPLORATION. The unknown holds such a fascination for man that the desire to explore must be counted among his basic drives. Whether it is going to the moon, climbing an unconquered mountain peak, or reading for the first time a recently-discovered scroll, man thrills to exploration. The preacher can assist in fulfillment of this drive by leading in activities and studies that carry the excitement of exploration. This thrill can come from testifying to someone who does not know the gospel; from bringing food and clothing to the needy; from helping a family find its bond of love; from bringing a sense of being wanted to a lonely widow, ex-convict, or one of a minority race. Too often Christian living is seen as dull, unexciting, and boring, so people turn elsewhere for exploration sometimes becoming so embroiled in the physical pursuit that they abandon the spiritual life entirely. Christ offers plenty of excitement and thrill if Christians but seek it in the right way.

RESPECT AND WORSHIP. Wherever mankind has been he has sought to worship something beyond himself. The archaeologist's spade reveals the objects of worship from every past civilization. For this need, Christianity provides the finest satisfaction: a God of love, a guide of truth, a goal of heaven. Every preacher should make full use of man's innate drive for something beyond himself as a basis for teaching how to build the right relationship with God.

These ten drives, then, summarize the fundamental, inborn needs and wants of every individual. While each will vary in its strength in different persons and even in the same person at different times or different stages of life, the preacher must understand these aspects of human nature and their relationship to Christian teaching. Frequently, his sermons should be focused on helping his congregation find the good fulfillment while avoiding "lust," desiring to go beyond God's limits for a drive and thus engaging in unrestrained pursuit of a drive.

SOLUTION TO EMOTIONAL PROBLEMS

Related to and growing from these drives are man's emotions, the third ingredient of the soil of men's needs. A rather abbreviated list of emotions includes: fear, hate, love, insecurity, anger, guilt, shame, pride, loneliness, worry, excitement, sorrow, pity, sympathy, humor, and inferiority. *These emotions may be regarded as the "feelings" man has about his drives.* One will, for example, fear that which threatens his self-preservation and love that which enhances it. He will hate that

which keeps him from attaining power, take pride in his possessions, sorrow when his affections are lost, and feel shame when
he offends those from whom he seeks approval. Excitement
accompanies those occasions when a sudden fulfillment is
anticipated or a sudden loss is feared.

While, as we shall see later,[2] a preacher will use motives and
emotions to persuade, he must also understand them so he can
help members of his congregation adjust to situations involving
their emotions.

Edgar Jackson, in his book *How to Preach to People's Needs,*
discusses such emotional needs as guilt feelings, sorrow, fear,
insecurity, alcoholism, loneliness, defeat, anger, doubt, ten-
sion, inferiority, and immaturity. He observes:

> On the basis of compilations of averages it may be
> possible to get some concept of a cross section of your
> congregation. In a congregation of five hundred people,
> it is reasonable to assume that at least one hundred have
> been so recently bereaved as to feel an acute sense of loss.
> Probably a third of the married persons are facing prob-
> lems of personality adjustment that may weaken or de-
> stroy their home life. At least half of the five hundred can
> be assumed to have problems of emotional adjustment at
> school, work, home, or community that endanger their
> happiness. Others may have neuroses ranging from alco-
> hol addiction to lesser forms of obsessions and anxiety
> states. Perhaps fifteen or more are homosexually inclined
> and another twenty-five depressed. Another hundred may
> be suffering from so great a feeling of guilt or fear of
> discovery that their peace of mind and health are jeopar-
> dized. The rare individual with complete peace of mind
> and soul is probably surrounded by those who are carrying
> several heavy burdens within.[3]

---

[2] This aspect of emotions and motives is covered in Chapter 6.

[3] Edgar N. Jackson, *How to Preach to People's Needs* (New York: Abingdon
Press, 1956), 14.

Though such statistics are virtually impossible to substantiate with exactness for a given congregation, they should open the eyes of most preachers to the emotional needs they face in the pulpit each Sunday.

In almost every audience some person will be in the midst of making a difficult decision and will need spiritual direction. Another will be in a spiritual crisis and, with the right guidance, can be directed into the kingdom. Some family on the verge of breakup may be turned back toward peace. Someone contemplating a sinful deed may be dissuaded.

All these drives and emotions are throbbing in the minds and hearts of the congregation. The problems and needs call for a skilled physician who can apply the healing Word of God.

SPECIFIC SPIRITUAL NEEDS

In addition to these fundamental spiritual needs that lie in human nature, there are specific spiritual needs that a preacher must recognize and help to meet. If we think of the preacher's role as one of helping pilgrims on a journey to heaven, these specific spiritual needs might be divided into several categories.

1. *Helping travelers to find the right road.* While there are those who profess to believe that "all roads lead to heaven," such is clearly not the biblical view. Peter declared that "salvation is found in no one else" but Jesus Christ (Acts 4:12), and the Bible's constant warning against false teachers makes it clear that a wrong road is not as good as the right one. Jesus, using this very road analogy, said that most would follow the broad way to destruction while only a few would walk the narrow road to life (Matthew 7:13).

So the preacher must help people find the right road and that means he must preach, as early Christian preachers did, about the kingdom of God and how to enter it through the new birth. No preacher can follow the New Testament model for preaching without preaching *evangelistic sermons* that teach listeners who are not on the road to heaven how to get on it and then urging them to get on it.

2. *Helping travelers on the right road to know how to walk*

on it. John taught those who had found the right road that they must "walk in the light" (1 John 1:7). Walking in the light means that our aim is to be as much like God as possible for John continued that we are to "walk in the light as he [God] is in the light."

Preachers, then, must help travelers to model their lives after God's qualities, particularly as they were demonstrated by God in the flesh. Sermons must help to develop a Christlike personality, the spirit of service, and high moral standards.

John's teaching is that one who is striving to walk in the light will sin occasionally and that such sins are forgiven by the blood of Christ. But he also warns that Christians may leave the road of light for the road of darkness (1 John 1:6).

3. *Helping travelers with their relationships with others.* A very important aspect of life on the road to heaven is the relationship one has with others. In regard to this, the preacher should deal with those personal qualities that contribute to getting along well with and understanding others. Family relations are another important element since most travelers will be making this trip in family units and since the Bible has so much to say that can be of help to husbands, wives, parents, and children. Since God has also directed that travelers gather in congregations, he has given instructions for relationships in these groups, too.

4. *Helping travelers in their relationship with God.* Even though one is traveling the road to heaven, he/she must not forget to maintain the right relationship with God—the Father, Son, and Holy Spirit. So the preacher should help his pilgrims (1) to worship God well, (2) to develop an increasingly close personal relationship to Jesus, and (3) to sense a meaningful relationship to the Holy Spirit whom God gives those who are heaven bound as a sign of His presence with them.

5. *Helping travelers to live by God's priorities.* One of the great temptations to pilgrims on the road to heaven is to become diverted from their main destination to secondary matters. Sometimes these diversions are to engage in something beyond God's limits; but, perhaps even more often, the diversion is something that is not sinful in itself. Satan knows that a job, a

hobby, a person, a recreation, a possession can be important enough to obscure the vision of the traveler, causing him/her to miss the way and, thus, to leave the heavenly walk entirely. The preacher, then, must help those he can influence to "seek first the kingdom of heaven."

6. *Helping travelers to serve others.* No one can successfully make the trip to heaven who is selfishly focused on his/her own interests. The spirit of service which so permeated the life of Jesus must also characterize those walking to meet Him. This service certainly includes sharing with others the good news about how to get on the road and how to continue there. It also includes serving Christ through the work of His body, the church, serving family, and serving any in need, as did the Samaritan on the Jericho road. The preacher must exemplify, encourage, and equip travelers in service.

If a preacher will, then, keep before him the image of helping travelers on the road to heaven, he will be able to keep his focus on the wide variety of spiritual needs he needs to serve with his ministry.

CLOSING OBSERVATIONS

In addition to these basic needs, there are, of course, those *specific problems which face particular congregations*—and of these the preacher must be conscious. There are occasions when members are in conflict with each other and need to be admonished, "Let there be no divisions among you" (1 Corinthians 1:10). There are times when the program needs stimulation and the congregation needs to be told "I can do all things in Him that strengtheneth me" (Philippians 4:13). Moments of international strife require the preacher to recall the words of the psalmist, "God is our refuge and strength, a very present help in trouble" (Psalms 41:1). Those inclined to doubt must be reminded that "These things are written that ye might believe, and that believing ye might have life in his name" (John 20:31). There are particular needs of youth, of the elderly, and other specific groups of which the preacher also needs to be aware.

It is obvious that preaching demands a knowledge of individual needs, a knowledge far more specific than those given by general observations or statistics. A preacher must know his congregation from firsthand contact, from visiting in their homes, businesses, and schools. He must be with them in work and play as well as in the classroom and pulpit. He must know the community through its news media and contact with community leaders. He must be acquainted with local, state, national, and international events for illustration and application, but most of all for understanding the temper of the times and the state of the people. He should look through records of the church, become acquainted with its history and learn of its progress. Indeed a preacher must be a close student of both his Book and his people.

Many great preachers have given testimony to the need of knowing the congregation. William Taylor, who delivered the Lyman Beecher Lectures on Preaching in 1876, suggested four avenues by which the minister might learn man: "The study of the many characters of the Bible, which, he said represent 'every phase of human nature.' The second area of source material was the field of human literature or history. The third source of information indicated by Taylor was 'the dramatic works of Shakespeare.' His final suggestion was 'to mingle much among men themselves.'"[4] Henry Ward Beecher advised:

> Begin your ministry with the common people. Get seasoned with the humanity and sympathies which belong to men; mix with farmers, mechanics and laboring men; eat with them, sleep with them; for after all, there is the great substance of humanity.[5]

Jesus spoke of Himself as a physician who came to heal the sick souls of men; preachers who follow their Master are physicians also. The Holy Spirit has provided a great store of drugs for numerous types of illness, so the preacher must

---

[4] Batsell Barrett Baxter, *The Heart of the Yale Lectures* (New York: Macmillan Co., 1947), 241, 242. Quoted in part from William M. Taylor, *The Ministry of the Word* (London: T. Nelson and Sons, 1876), 41-44.

[5] Henry Ward Beecher, *Yale Lectures on Preaching*, 3 vols. (New York: Charles Scribner's Sons, 1890), 147; quoted in Baxter, 243.

examine his patient, diagnose the disease, and apply the remedy. Knowledge of the divine remedies is required, but this alone is insufficient. The preacher must understand his patients and know their problems, and then, as carefully as a skilled neurosurgeon removes a defective portion of the brain, he must seek to apply exactly the right remedy in the most effective manner.

The key to meeting the needs of the congregation, then, is to make preaching relevant. While we preach an ancient gospel, it is still applicable to the modern world. It deals with basic problems among men and between man and God. The way to make preaching relevant is not to abandon the old gospel but to make it meaningful in terms of current problems, longing, and needs. Two of the amazing qualities of the Scriptures, indeed, are both their timeliness and their timelessness.

Perhaps the best advice which can be given to most preachers is that the audience always asks, "So what?" "So what if David sinned with Bathsheba?" "So what if there are different kinds of love?" "So what if God is love?" "So what if God said His people should be modest or tell the truth?" Every sermon should leave each hearer saying, "I know how this applies to me." The "So what?" of the sermon was that I should know this or do that or change in this way. The tendency of most of us, if we make any application at all, is to apply a teaching to someone else. The preacher, thus, must not only preach to a need but must be certain that the listeners make the application to their own lives.

Any minister who can "put the brethren in mind" of what they truly need and can help them apply it to their lives will render a service of eternal importance.

ASSIGNMENT

Preaching to Needs

Write a paper of not more than 1,500 words dealing with the topics following:

1. How would you discover the information you need to analyze the needs of a congregation to which you have just moved?

2. List and explain briefly what you believe to be the five most basic needs in most congregations today.

3. Analyze a particular congregation, noting both its general characteristics and specific needs. (This part should be carefully and thoughtfully done since a later assignment will depend on it.)

4. List six sermon topics you could preach which would help your congregation deal with any one inborn drive of your choice.

5 | Varying the Functions Of the Sermon

"Reprove, rebuke, exhort, with all longsuffering and teaching" — 2 Timothy 4:2

INTRODUCTION

Undoubtedly some of the finest advice for preachers is found in letters which Paul, a seasoned veteran, wrote to the neophyte Timothy, and a very important part of this advice deals with the need for sermons designed to achieve different purposes. Paul instructed: *"Preach the word; be urgent in season, out of season; reprove, rebuke, exhort, with all longsuffering and teaching" (2 Timothy 4:2).* There are, he says, times to reprove and rebuke, and there are times to exhort and teach. Only two verses before, Paul had suggested that the Scriptures are profitable for "teaching, for reproof, for correction, for instruction which is in righteousness: that the man of God may be complete, furnished completely unto every good work" (2 Timothy 3:16, 17).

As indicated in Chapter 4, the preacher must preach to needs, but in doing so he must plan a balanced program of sermons just as a general maps his strategy for storming an enemy strong-hold. A minister usually preaches to his congregation a hundred times a year, and over a period of several years has the opportunity to present basic themes to meet their needs. He must, however, include variations in his approach and his purposes, for, if he speaks too often on the same theme, he draws a negative response from the audience which first tires of and then jokes about his "hobby." If he deals only with the simple matters of the gospel, he "stunts" the growth of his congregation by giving them milk only; if he feeds them on a constant diet of meat, many may starve because they can neither chew nor digest the food provided. The minister may view his selection of general themes, then, like a weaver making a tapestry. Over a period of time, his sermons should form a well designed pattern.

The preacher, then, will first *discover the needs of the congregation*; then he must *diagnose specific and immediate problems* of those whom he serves; and finally, he must *devise a program* of preaching which will both meet these needs and gain a favorable reception from the congregation.

To change the metaphor, a preacher seeks to develop each member of his congregation in continual growth much like the nurseryman grows his trees. *A tree grows in four ways at one time: roots, trunk and branches, leaves, and fruit.* The Christian, likewise, grows in four ways at one time: *knowledge, convictions, inspiration, and action.*

The root or foundation of the Christian's growth is *knowledge.* Peter indicated that one must "grow in the grace and *knowledge of* our Lord and Savior Jesus Christ" (2 Peter 3:18), and he listed *knowledge as* one of the Christian graces (2 Peter 1:5-6). Jesus, likewise, placed knowledge at the base of Christian growth when he said, "It is written in the prophets, and *they shall all be taught of God.* Every one, therefore, that hath heard from the Father, *and hath learned,* cometh unto me" (John 6:45). The Great Commission emphasizes the same point: "Go ye, therefore, and *make disciples [learners]* of all nations, baptizing them in the name of the Father, Son and Holy Spirit, teaching them to observe all things whatsoever I have commanded you" (Matthew 28:18-19). Any follower of Jesus who does not grow in knowledge will wither and die just as the people of Hosea's day. "My people," he said, "are destroyed for lack of knowledge" (Hosea 4:6). *Knowledge, then, like the tree's roots, supplies the nourishment which makes growth in the other parts possible.*

The church in Pergamum provides an example of a congregation which lacked sufficient knowledge. Although Jesus commended them for "holding fast" to certain beliefs, because of their ignorance on other issues they had allowed false teaching and were, therefore, charged to "repent or else" (Revelation 2:12-17).

Christians must, above all, know the Scriptures which make them "wise unto salvation," and they must be able to apply them to their own times and circumstances. Put another way, they must know Christ *and* His teachings.

From the roots of knowledge grows *the trunk of conviction.* A Christian is not merely one who knows; he is also one who *believes*. John stated the purpose of much of the Bible, saying, "These things are written that ye might believe" (John 20:31). The writer of Hebrews defines faith as "assurance of things hoped for, a conviction of things not seen" (Hebrews 11:1). Stated in other terms, *faith is that quality which gives reality to what Christians hope for but cannot see.* The Christian's conviction makes God, Christ, heaven, and all other spiritual concepts to be actual and real to him. Faith in God is the sturdy trunk of life, and conviction about various truths of the gospel constitutes the branches. Stimulating the growth of all these convictions is the work of every preacher.

The leaves on this tree are inspiration. A tree may have good roots and a large trunk, but without leaves it will die. As sunlight upon the leaves makes them produce food for the tree, so the preacher's sermons must inspire the Christian, thus producing fuel for his growth and productivity.

Many a Christian, unfortunately, stands like a dead tree with the roots of knowledge and the trunk and branches of conviction about Bible doctrines, but without life or fruit. A Christian with knowledge and conviction but without feeling, love, or zeal is fit only to be burned for he/she is incomplete and useless.

The church at Ephesus demonstrates the importance of inspiration. Jesus praised them for refusing false teachers and for bearing tribulation, but He condemned them for leaving their "first love." In spite of their stand for sound doctrines, their failure to love and act caused Jesus to warn: "Remember therefore whence thou art fallen, and repent and do the first works, or else I come to thee, and will move thy candlestick out of its place" (Revelation 2:5).

Finally, every good tree produces fruit. This was a favorite illustration of Jesus: the barren fig tree was cursed; the unfruitful branches were cut off the vine and cast into the fire; and the "fruit test" was suggested as a means of distinguishing between false and true prophets. The preacher, then, must work for action. *Fruitbearing* is the real test of discipleship, for "every branch in me that beareth not fruit, he taketh it away" (John 15:2). In every example Jesus gave of the judgment, moreover, He used those who bore no fruit as the sample of the doomed: the one talent man, the five foolish virgins, the unprepared guest at the marriage feast, and those who failed to help the needy. To the church at Sardis, Jesus wrote, ". . . thou hast a name that thou livest, but thou art dead. . . . for I have found no works of thine perfected before my God" (Revelation 3:1, 2). They were dead because no fruit had come to ripeness.

Knowledge, convictions, and inspiration, therefore, are designed as means to the end of fruitbearing and action. To know the teaching of the Bible on marriage is good, but to build a Christian home is better; to be convinced of the divinity of Jesus is good, but to lead others to the same conclusion is better; to understand the doctrine of the *logos* is good, but to live by and for the Word is better.

The aim, then, of the preacher is to produce in his hearers the qualities of knowledge, conviction, inspiration, and action. Each of these, like the four parts of a tree, grows simultaneously, and the growth in one part helps all the other parts for they are interrelated. One more similarity is also important: as long as a tree lives, it grows, and when it ceases to grow, it dies. Likewise, the Christian must grow continually and the preacher must understand this growth and make an important contribution to it.

Knowledge, conviction, inspiration, and action are each accomplished by a sermon planned for that particular purpose, and the sermons so designed are designated as sermons *to inform, to convince, to inspire, and to actuate.* These four types of sermons are, moreover, in an ascending order. The easiest to achieve is the imparting of information, and sermons to convince, inspire, and actuate become increasingly more difficult in that order. The more difficult type, *almost invariably, also necessitates achieving the aims below it.* Thus, the sermon to convince must first convey the information; the sermon to inspire must first inform and convince; and the sermon to actuate will likely inform, convince, and stimulate before stirring to action.

In addition to understanding each of these types of sermons, a preacher should also analyze each of these into more specific goals. The following list of general subject areas for each of these categories of sermons both explains further each of these sermon purposes and provides a broad list of subjects suitable for each type. These statements also provide a good overview for a minister's long-range aims for his ministry with a congregation and should be reviewed frequently as a check on the balance of topics for sermons. Each topic listed, of course, would be subdivided into many individual sermons. All of these taken together would form a balanced diet for a congregation over a period of years.

Discussion Question: What balance should a preacher seek between sermons of each of the four types?

PURPOSES FOR PREACHING

The preacher should inform the congregation of:

1. The biblical story of man from creation through the establishment and early growth of the church including the periods of Bible history, the dispensations of God's dealing with men, the lives of Bible characters, and the geography of Bible lands.

2. The Bible, as an inspired communication from God, and

of the method God intended us to use in understanding and applying His Word.

3. God's plan for reconciling lost mankind: the fall, the promise, the law, the prophecies, the Christ, and the church.

4. The characteristics of deity and the nature and work of the Godhead: the Father, the Son, and the Holy Spirit.

5. The life and teachings of Jesus.

6. The establishment of the church, the plan for being born into it, its purpose and work, its organization, its discipline, its worship, its laws, and the responsibilities of membership.

7. The great Bible doctrines such as law and grace, faith and atonement, reconciliation, the new birth, and the kingdom.

8. The traits of character which the Christian must develop.

9. The value of the soul and the needs of the lost.

10. The origin and work of Satan and the nature and folly of sin.

11. The great blessings and advantages of being a Christian.

12. Marriage, the home as God would have it, and the responsibilities, opportunities, and means of being good participants in the various roles of family life.

13. The fundamental beliefs of prominent religious groups of the world.

14. The work of Christians in caring for the poor, the bereaved, and the spiritually destitute both at home and abroad.

15. The various methods and techniques of Bible study.

16. The application of Christian principles to social, political, and business affairs.

The preacher should convince the congregation that:

1. God is, that He made the world, that He has been and is concerned about man.

2. Jesus was "in the beginning," that the "Word" became flesh, that He was born of a virgin, that He worked miracles and taught, that He died on the cross and was raised from the dead.

3. The Bible is the infallible, inspired Word of God written by men who were Spirit-filled for men who were sin-filled.

4. There is a heaven for the righteous and a hell for the wicked.

5. The Scriptures are sufficient for man's spiritual needs, that all biblical teachings intended for men today must be obeyed, and that religious doctrines either not supported by or opposed by the Scriptures are error and to be avoided.

6. Spiritual matters are as real as physical and are of infinitely greater value.

7. Christianity is the finest way to meet man's need and to solve his problems.

The preacher should inspire the congregation:

1. To worship privately and publicly in a meaningful and acceptable way.

2. To increase constantly their love for God and Christ, for fellow Christians, and for the lost.

3. To have a growing faith and hope.

4. To grow more like Christ daily.

5. To train for greater service.

6. To have zeal for visiting and serving others both physically and spiritually.

7. To have greater love for good and more hatred for evil.

8. To be better parents and children, husbands and wives.

9. To have greater enthusiasm for the Lord and to sacrifice more time, money, and talents for His kingdom.

10. To be a consolation in bereavement, sorrow, and affliction.

11. To live in accordance with one's convictions.

12. To be loyal to the local congregation and its elders.

13. To have an appreciation of their Christian heritage.

The preacher should actuate the congregation:

1. To become Christians (if not already).

2. To participate in immediate programs such as vacation Bible school, a visitation program, a special donation, a series of meetings, home Bible studies, a benevolent work.

3. To attend the services of the church and Bible classes regularly.

4. To read the Bible and pray daily.

5. To confess sin or reject a sinful practice.

6. To live above the world and to be a good example.

7. To choose one's ministry in the kingdom, to prepare for it, and to be active in its work.

8. To assist in some specific task: send a missionary, appoint deacons, start a building program.

9. To vote in accordance with God's will when a political issue is inextricably tied to moral and religious principles.

10. To participate in community activities which afford an opportunity for Christian service.

From these lists, it will be observed that the goals for inspiration are primarily those which stir to feeling and attitudes while sermons to actuate aim at a more specific overt response. The goals of conviction deal with beliefs and doctrines. Sermons to inform present a well-rounded knowledge of the teachings of the Scriptures and their relationship to man's needs.

The aims listed above are far too broad, of course, to be the aim of a single sermon, but when each preacher has expanded these lists and made them his own, every sermon which he delivers should find its place in assisting him to accomplish one of the goals he believes should be a part of his ministry. A hundred sermons or more can and should be preached, over a period of time, on many of the long-range goals listed. An occasional review of this, or a similar list, will assist a preacher in knowing what areas he may be neglecting and in suggesting topics he may need to preach on.

STATING THE PURPOSE

For every sermon the preacher prepares, he should have a clear, concise statement of purpose. Without this careful focus on a specific target, he will find that his sermons may be enjoyable to hear but bring no change in lives.

This statement of purpose should have these elements: (1) identification of the type of sermon, (2) statement of the general content to be presented, and (3) a statement of the specific outcome the preacher is seeking. The general purpose of the sermon should be "to inform," "to convince," "to inspire," or "to actuate." The purpose statement should always begin with one of these aims so that the basic type of sermon he is preparing will be firmly established in the preacher's mind. He will think in a different mode, for example, if the sermon is to inform or to stimulate.

The second element of the purpose sentence, written near the top of the outline, should spell out more specifically the content of the sermon. The third, and most important part of the purpose statement gives the specific response the preacher hopes each listener will make. With this outcome stated specifically, the preacher is far more likely to develop a sermon which will achieve the result he is seeking.

Some examples of purpose statements for a sermon to inform are:

1. To inform the congregation of the meaning of redemption so that they will wish to accept it or to share it with others.

2. To inform the congregation of the responsibilities of elders so that they will make a good selection of men to serve in this role.

3. To inform the congregation of the teaching of Christ on divorce and remarriage so that those married will seek to stay married and those not married will choose carefully.

Some examples of purpose statements for sermons to convince are:

1. To convince the non-Christian that Jesus is divine and the Christian that his/her faith is well founded so that he/she will develop a stronger faith in Jesus.

2. To convince the congregation that Matthew 24 does not give signs by which to determine when the end of the world will be so that he/she will not be troubled by false teaching on this topic and can explain his/her belief to others.

3. To convince the audience that the saved can be lost so that they will want to live carefully as Christians.

Some examples of purpose statements for sermons to inspire are:

1. To inspire the congregation to a deeper feeling when

participating in the Lord's Supper so that their participation will be acceptable and uplifting.

2. To inspire the congregation to greater love for one another so that they will do more to help each other with their needs.

3. To inspire non-members to a sense of appreciation for the joys of Christian living so that they will want to accept Jesus' way.

Some examples of purpose statements for sermons to actuate are:

1. To actuate the members of the congregation to do personal work so that they will volunteer for a personal-work program starting next week.

2. To actuate non-members to accept Christ so they will become Christians immediately.

3. To actuate members to a greater spirit of sacrifice so they will give as God has prospered them.

Occasionally, it will seem appropriate to combine two purposes into one sermon: to convince the congregation that a home Bible study program is needed and to actuate them to volunteer to work in it. In most cases, however, the lower level objective is encompassed in the higher and the double statement is not necessary.

The more specific and direct the statement of purpose, and the more observable an act it suggests, the more likely it is that the sermon will achieve its goal. Preachers would often improve their preaching tremendously by the simple device of writing out in the purpose statement exactly what they hope to achieve with the sermon. What do they hope the audience will do with the message? How will their lives be different? What sins will they avoid? What Christian graces will they exhibit? What work for the Lord will they do? How will their lives, their jobs, their homes, their church be better? By carefully crafting the purpose sentence the preacher will be stating exactly the "*So what?*" he hopes to reach.

This specific statement of the outcome not only helps the aim but it also provides the basis for measuring the extent to which the preacher achieved his goal. Of course, some goals are long-range and will not be seen in a day or week or month, but others can be measured more quickly or, at least, some observable trend may be noted.

REVIEW

The first three steps in preparing a sermon should now be clear. Any one of these steps may come first, depending upon the specific circumstances, but they usually occur in this order: (1) analysis of the audience to determine the needs, both immediate and long range; (2) the choice of the purposes to be achieved over an extended period of time and specifically in one sermon; and finally, (3) the selection of a specific sermon subject which will help to achieve one of the aims which the preacher sets.

In some cases, particularly when speaking on a special occasion of some type, the subject may be designated for the preacher; but in the normal case, he will select his own topic. This choice must not be made without consideration of his analysis of the audience's needs and his plan for purposes to be achieved over a given period of time. A very fine practice is for a preacher to work out a list of sermons to be used over a two- or three-month period. This practice will help him to keep in mind the proper balance between all the purposes he seeks to achieve and, unless such a plan is followed, he may look back on the list of sermons he has preached only to find that his whole program has been to inform or to actuate and too little variety has been used. (See Chapter 3 for more on sermon subjects.)

The immediate and long-range goals of the preacher should always be in the "back of his mind," so he can choose wisely the specific topics which will fit into his overall plan. His contact with the people in all types of circumstances should provide the stimulus for a host of sermon topics suited to the congregation's needs. Some specific seasons of the year, a local, national, or international event, and church events will also give ideas for specific sermons.

Discussion Question: To what extent should the preacher plan sermons to correspond to special times of the year like New Year's Day, Easter, Memorial Day, 4th of July, Labor

Day, Thanksgiving, Christmas, etc.?

It should also be pointed out, of course, that a given purpose may be achieved in many ways. Suppose that a minister's purpose is to actuate the congregation to increase the contribution. He may, of course, build a sermon which comes right to the point, "You should give more because. . . ." But he may find a subtle approach more effective in accomplishing the same purpose. He might, for example, preach on "giving as an act of worship," or on "stewardship," "liberality," "the generosity of the Macedonians," "the offerings of the Jews," or any one of a hundred other topics—all designed to accomplish the same general purpose.

Audience analysis, the choice of the purpose, and selection of the subject, then, are the first steps in the preparation of a sermon and these must lay the proper foundation for that which follows.

ASSIGNMENT

Varying the Functions of the Sermon

1. Plan sermons you would preach for six weeks (twelve sermons) to the specific congregation you analyzed earlier. Make these sermons to meet the needs you stated with clearly stated objectives and balance them between sermons to inform, to convince, to stimulate, and to actuate. Begin to choose the topics now, but do not develop them until the next unit which will deal with sermon organization. The assignment will be due then.

2. Prepare for class delivery a sermon of ten minutes in length. This sermon should be outlined as indicated in Chapter 3 and have a carefully crafted statement of purpose, subject sentence, and main headings. It may be a sermon of any type but should be designed to meet a specific need.

6 | Organizing Material And Using Sermon Plans

"Handling aright the word of truth"
— 2 Timothy 2:15

INTRODUCTION

Every speech theorist since the days of Plato and Aristotle has testified to the importance of organizing the materials to be spoken. The ancients called it *disposition* or *arrangement* and thought of it in terms of the *strategy* a general might use in deploying his troops. While no one denies the need for a well-organized sermon, many do not give sufficient importance to it. Some, for example, would consider the organization sufficient as long as the speaker gathers into one place all he has to say on a given point. As we shall see, however, far more than this is involved.

Developing the proper structure for a sermon requires: (1) the *choice of the central theme* of the sermon and the *main points*, (2) the *support* of each of these main points, (3) the *order* in which the main points are to appear, (4) *transitions* from one idea to the next, (5) the *introduction* and *conclusion* for the sermon, and (6) the development of the *climax*.

Whether a sermon is designed to inform, convince, stimulate or actuate, *the fundamental message of the speech is a series of related ideas or points*. The points may state the basic information to be learned, the beliefs to be supported, or the acts to be performed. Such statements form the skeleton or basic outline of the speech. Careful attention to organizing these basic points will make the sermon both "preachable" and "listenable." Well-developed points can more easily be remembered by both the speaker and the audience. Nothing is more disconcerting to a listener than to sit for thirty minutes and hear 4,500 words thrown at him with nothing in any apparent order. How frustrating to hear examples, testimony, and factual data without knowing to what key point each is attached. Since the human mind is designed to understand and appreciate that which has order, design, and balance, the preacher will find careful organization of materials one of his most potent weapons.

THE SUBJECT SENTENCE

If the structure of a sermon is viewed as a missile, the warhead the missile delivers is the *subject sentence*, or to use other terms, the *proposition* or the *thesis*. In every sermon the preacher should seek to "shoot" some fundamental message or basic truth into the minds of his congregation. Just as propelling the warhead is the whole purpose of the missile, so everything in the sermon seeks to "drive home" the subject sentence which expresses what the preacher desires the audience to know, believe, feel, or do.

The subject sentence, then, becomes the focal point of the structure; it is the hub of the wheel, the point of the arrow, and the fullback for whom every other player blocks so he can score the touchdown. All the other parts of the speech—main points, introduction, conclusion, supporting material—are designed to make the subject sentence hit the target. In a sermon to *inform*, for example, the subject sentence might be:

Subject Sentence: David was a man after God's own heart.

Main Points of Body:
  I. David's defeat of Goliath showed his complete trust in God.
  II. David's refusal to kill Saul showed his complete acceptance of the purposes of God.
  III. David's repentance after his sin showed his complete submission to God.

These three points blend together in the statement that David was a man after God's own heart, and each point develops one aspect of the subject sentence.

In a speech to *convince*, the subject sentence is the *proposition to be proved*:

Subject Sentence: Jesus is the Christ.
Main Points of Body:
  I. Jesus' fulfillment of prophecy proves Him to be the Christ.
  II. Jesus' miracles prove Him to be the Christ.
  III. Jesus' resurrection proves Him to be the Christ.

When the preacher's purpose is to *stimulate*, the subject sentence expresses *the theme which he believes will inspire the audience*:

Subject Sentence: Christians get the most satisfaction out of life.
Main Points of Body:
  I. Christians enjoy life through freedom from the burdens of pride, malice, and worry.
  II. Christians enjoy life through service to others.
  III. Christians enjoy life through fellowship with God and His people.

Finally, in the sermon to *actuate*, the subject sentence is often the action asked for: "Visit the sick," "Read the Bible daily," "Increase your offering," "Attend Bible School." On many occasions, however, the preacher will find a better response by using a less direct approach. If he wishes to actuate the congregation to greater participation in the church program, for example, he might preach on the church at Laodicea:

Subject Sentence: Jesus' letter to the church at Laodicea indicates His reaction to unemployed church members.
Main Points of Body:
  I.   Jesus knew the church was lukewarm and self-satisfied.
  II. Jesus offered a remedy for their condition.
  III. Jesus promised great blessings conditioned upon their acceptance of His terms.

The first step in organizing the sermon, then, is to determine the subject sentence, the warhead to be delivered. It should be worded in a striking, concise, memorable fashion so it can be easily grasped by the audience.

THE MAIN POINTS OF THE BODY

Once the subject sentence is stated, the next essential part of the organization is to *develop main points which will support it*. These provide the structure for the "body" or "discussion" of the sermon. The body will be made up of a series of units, each of which is constructed of two parts: (1) a *statement* or main point and (2) its accompanying *supporting material*. This *statement* or *assertion* and its *accompanying* Scriptures, facts, or examples, then, make up a *basic unit*; and it is of such units that the body of the speech is composed. Usually these are designated in outline form such as:

I. Statement or	A. Statement
A. Support	1. Support
B. Support	2. Support

Since supporting material is the subject of the next chapter, the concern here is with the statements of points which form the skeleton of the sermon. How does the preacher determine what main points to use in support of his subject sentence? How many such points should he use, and in what order?

Determining the Main Points

Since the entire body of the speech may be regarded as the development or support of the subject sentence, the *main points of the body are, in reality, divisions of the subject sentence*. If, for example, a preacher's subject sentence is "Have this mind in you, which was also in Christ Jesus," the audience naturally expects the body of the sermon to be built around the particular traits of mind which characterized Jesus: humility, obedience, sacrifice (Philippians 2:2-10). As *divisions of the subject sentence*, then, these become the *main points of the body* of the sermon.

While an active mind usually has little difficulty in finding a suitable method for analyzing the subject sentence into some set of reasonable divisions, there are a number of *patterns* which may be laid over the subject sentence to simplify the process of cutting it into pieces. As in dressmaking, too, these pieces are then sewn back together to make up the body of the speech.

As we consider the step of providing the skeleton for the sermon, let us begin with a consideration of two fundamental types of sermons: (1) *passage-based* approaches and (2) *subject-based* approaches. A *passage-based* sermon starts with a verse, a group of verses, a chapter, or a book of the Bible and analyzes that passage so as to develop a message to meet the needs of the audience. A *subject-based sermon*, on the other hand, begins with a topic rather than a passage and analyzes the teaching of the Scripture on that topic from many passages. Of course, a verse may have suggested the topic, but if the preacher intends to focus on the subject rather than the verse, then he is using the subject-based approach.

Note at the very beginning that both of these types are Scripture-based: one starts with a particular passage of Scripture and develops its organization upon an analysis of that passage while the other analyzes the topic from light shed on it from a number of passages. Neither is necessarily more biblical than the other.

Both of these types of sermons have an important place. Certainly it is useful, at times, to preach on such subjects as faith, conversion, conscience, courage, repentance, the God-head, and many other subjects. On other occasions, however, one may well build a sermon on 1 Corinthians 13, the Beati-tudes, Isaiah 53, Genesis 1:1, or many other passages. No preacher should be without the capacity to preach both types of sermons, and no preacher should limit himself to only one style of sermon for that will not allow him the best way to meet all needs.

Notice as each type is considered, how main points must be worded in a parallel fashion. Polishing the wording until head-ings match each other is vital. If the preacher cannot find a way to make them parallel in wording, then they do not have an equal standing with the subject sentence and he must keep working until they do. Also, concise, pungent, parallel statements are much more easily grasped and retained by the audience.

1. *Passage-based Sermons.* First, let us look at *passage-based sermons*—those which start with a particular verse or section of Scripture. We may divide this type into four major sub-types: Textual, Expository I, Expository II, and Explained-Exemplified-Applied. All of these start with a single passage as a focal point but each treats it in a different way.

a. *Textual.* A textual sermon has two fundamental character-istics: (1) it typically treats only *one* or *two* verses of Scripture, usually taking some portion of them as its subject sentence, and (2) it takes *exact words* or *phrases* from those verses as the main headings of the sermon.

Thus we find in 1 Timothy 4:12, "Let no man despise thy youth; but be thou an ensample to them that believe, in word, in manner of life, in love, in faith, in purity." This verse very naturally fits the textual sermon because a subject sentence (or main thrust) is easily seen in the statement "Be thou an ensample to the believers," and the words or phrases that follow naturally elaborate on this theme as main points. So a textual sermon outline on this verse would look like this:

Subject Sentence: Be thou an example to the believers.
Main Points of Body:
   I. In Word

   II. In Manner of Life
  III. In Love
  IV. In Faith
   V. In Purity

Each of these points, then, would be expanded with explanation, other Scriptures, and practical examples of the principle in action.

This type of sermon works especially well when there is a series of terms such as the works of the flesh (Galatians 5:19-21), the fruits of the spirit (Galatians 5:22, 23), the qualifications for elders (1 Timothy 3:2-7), or the Christian graces (2 Peter 1:5-7).

The textual sermon can also be quite effective in presenting a verse of Scripture that has two or three similar elements. First John 2:16, for example, speaks of the "lust of the flesh, the lust of the eyes, and the pride of life." Each of these could be a main division of this verse to support the subject sentence in the previous verse: "Love not the world."

Another example of a textual sermon could come from Romans 8:28. This familiar verse could be preached textually like this:

Subject Sentence: God works everything for good to the called who love Him.
   Main Points of Body:
     I. All things work together for good.
    II. To those who love God and are called according to His purpose.

The *first* point would be expanded to discuss *what* it means for all things to work together for good. This should include examples of this principle at work in the Bible and today. The *second* point would describe to *whom* God has made this promise. Who are the "called" and who are those who "love God"?

One more example of a textual sermon might come from Genesis 1:1 where each word or phrase of the verse could become a major section of the sermon.

Subject Sentence: "In the beginning God created the heaven and the earth."
Main Points of Body:
    I. "In the Beginning"
   II. "God"
  III. "Created"
  IV. "The Heavens and the Earth"

In each of the above examples, the textual sermon is seen to deal with a short passage (one or two verses) and it takes *the actual words or phrases in those verses as main headings.* The subject sentence may also be words directly from the text, may be the entire short passage, or may be a summation of it.

There are, however, some possible difficulties with the textual sermon. (1) Not all passages lend themselves to this type of treatment without being contrived and unnatural. Preachers often joke about someone who has preached a textual sermon by taking every word in the verse and making a point on it: "*Now*"; "Now *I*"; "Now I *beseech*"; "Now I beseech *you*"; "Now I beseech you, *brethren*"; and on and on *ad nauseam*. (2) One must also beware of taking a text out of its setting and making it mean something not intended by the writer. In 1 Corinthians 14:15, for example, Paul writes, "I will sing with the spirit, and I will sing with the understanding also." One might easily develop a textual sermon on (1) singing with the spirit and (2) singing with the understanding; but unless the context were carefully studied, he might easily fail to note that the use of spiritual gifts in the worship was the point under consideration, which gives the verse a very different meaning than that which appears when the verse is taken alone. (3) Still another danger of the textual sermon is that it may lack unity. Although several points may come from one verse, attention must still be given to developing unity among the points. If, for example, one should develop a textual sermon from Matthew 5:5: "Blessed are the meek, for they shall inherit the earth," he must develop the two points in relation to each other, thus avoiding two separated sermons, one on being meek, and another on inheriting the earth.

b. *Expository I.* Expository preaching has made a resurgence in recent times and, in many cases, that means a preacher is doing preaching that is closer to Scripture. There are, however, many definitions of expository preaching—one writer lists as many as twenty-five.

Some think expository preaching is reading a verse and then explaining it, then reading another verse and explaining it, and so on through a chapter. Others consider expository preaching to be explaining a passage and then giving applications of it.

Actually, the most useful view of expository preaching is to consider it as a sermon developed from three essential steps: (1) choose a section of Scripture, usually a paragraph, which appears to be a unit; (2) study the passage carefully to find its basic theme, message, lesson, or proposition to use as a subject sentence; and (3) find the main points that this passage teaches about the theme. In the expository sermon, the preacher usually will not use the exact words of the passage for the main points, as in the textual sermon, although the exact words may be used if they fit well. The analysis, however, is based on developing the theme as presented in the passage and not on the use of the actual words in the text.

A way of viewing an expository sermon is to think of the basic theme of the passage as a net which will be drawn through the passage to catch the lessons or points the passage reveals on that theme.

The most basic form of the expository sermon, which we are calling Expository I, takes as its theme the *fundamental theme which the author would have considered its fundamental thrust.* Notice how Henry Drummond used this approach for his famous sermon on 1 Corinthians 13. He took *love* as his theme for this sermon and developed it like this:

Subject Sentence: Love is the greatest thing in the world because of:
Main Points of Body:
   I.   The Importance of Love (vv. 1-3)

II.   The Nature of Love (vv. 4-7)

III. The Endurance of Love (vv. 8-13)

One could go even further with this passage to recognize that 1 Corinthians 13 is part of Paul's discussion of spiritual gifts (chapters 12—14) and make more use of its broader context:

Subject Sentence: The way of love is greater than the way of spiritual gifts.

Main Points of Body:

I.   Love provides a better motive than spiritual gifts (vv. 1-3).

II.   Love provides more help in Christian living than spiritual gifts (vv. 4-7).

III. Love provides more lasting benefits than spiritual gifts (vv. 8-13).

Note how the expository sermon is built entirely out of a single passage. The subject sentence and main headings all come from an analysis of one. While other passages and information from outside the Bible may be used in the development of a main heading, in the expository sermon the basic structure all comes entirely from the passage under consideration.

A study of Ephesians 5:22—6:9, to give another sample of an Expository I sermon, will reveal that the fundamental theme is "subjection," and that three relationships are "hung" on that theme—wives in subjection to husbands, children in subjection to parents, and slaves in subjection to masters. An outline of such a sermon would look like this:

Subject Sentence: Accept your responsibility in every relationship of life:

Main Points of Body:

I.   Husband/Wife

II.   Parent/Child

III. Master/Slave (Employer/Employee)

Some other samples of expository analysis are:

James 1:2-3, 12-15

Subject Sentence: Temptation can be a blessing or a curse.
Main Points of Body:
   I. The *source* of temptation is not God but our own lust.
  II. The *response* to temptation may be endurance or sin.
 III. The *outcome* of temptation may be patience or death.

Revelation 20:11-15

Subject Sentence: At the resurrection all will face God in judgment.
Main Points of Body:
   I. God's judgment is certain.
  II. God's judgment is based on our deeds.
 III. God's judgment allows mercy to some.
  IV. God's judgment is final.
   V. God's judgment is eternal.

An excellent example of the Expository I sermon was developed from Matthew 6:25-34 by R. Lofton Hudson in his book *The Religion of the Sound Mind*:

Subject Sentence: Christ teaches us how to stop worrying.
Main Points of Body:
   I. Value Yourself
      ("Are ye not of more value than birds and flowers?")
  II. Accept Yourself
      ("Which of you by being anxious can add one cubit?")
 III. Consecrate Yourself
      (Give yourself a cause—the kingdom of heaven.)

Notice how this sermon takes Jesus' central theme of "be not anxious" and analyzes His own suggestions into three parallel and powerful statements.

Parables are often used for Expository I sermons. The story

of the Good Samaritan, for example, has been preached like this:

Subject Sentence: The story of the Good Samaritan illustrates three philosophies of life.
Main Points of Body:
   I. The thieves said: "What's yours is mine, and I'll take it."
  II. The priest and Levite said: "What's mine is mine, and I'll keep it."
 III. The Samaritan said: "What's mine is yours, and I'll share it."

In each of these examples, a theme is chosen that reflects the basic thrust of the Bible writer. This theme becomes a string on which to hang points the passage makes about that theme.

c. *Expository II*. Now let us turn to Expository II sermons. Here the *analysis* is quite similar but, instead of using the *fundamental* theme of the passage, the preacher takes as the subject sentence a *secondary* theme in the passage or even a theme not mentioned directly in the passage but which the passage illuminates.

In Acts 2:1-13, for example, the central theme is the coming of the Holy Spirit on the apostles. One might, then, develop an Expository I sermon along that fundamental theme by speaking on (1) the *promise* of the Spirit (1:5-8; 2:16-21), (2) the *appearance* of the Spirit (2:1-4), and (3) the *results* of the Spirit (2:12).

But an Expository II sermon might take as a *secondary* theme of that same passage the act of *speaking in tongues*. Since this passage contains the only detailed description in the Scriptures of a tongue-speaking occasion, we may ask what we can learn here about speaking in tongues.

Subject Sentence: The tongue-speaking on Pentecost can teach us some very important lessons about the act of tongue speaking.
Main Points of Body:

   I.   Those who spoke in tongues were empowered by the Holy Spirit.

   II.   Those who spoke in tongues were speaking "known languages" they had never learned.

   III.   Those speaking in tongues were performing a sign to prove their new message was from God.

Another sample of an Expository II sermon comes from Acts 6. Here the main thrust is dealing with the problem of the Grecian widows. But a secondary theme is "church management."

Subject Sentence: The occasion of the first church dissension teaches us about church management.

Main Points of Body:

   I.   The apostles were aware of what the congregation thought and felt.

   II.   The apostles worked out a plan to present to all the people.

   III.   The apostles involved the people in solving the problem.

   IV.   The apostles delegated to others what they could.

   V.   The apostles continued to do what their own priorities demanded.

Another example of an Expository II sermon can be found in Romans 12:9-21. Here we find a list of admonitions for all Christians. These can be used in a special way, however, by taking the theme of elders, husbands, wives, employers, teachers, or children through this list. While the main thrust clearly makes this passage for all Christians, it takes on a special meaning when applied to Christians in particular situations to which it may be specifically applied. Such are secondary themes and so, when used as a subject sentence, the sermon is classified as Expository II.

Subject Sentence: Paul gives excellent advice to husbands and wives in Romans 12:9-13.

Main Points of Body:
  I. Let your love be pure.
  II. Reject evil in your home while holding fast to good.
  III. Work in your family roles with diligence.
  IV. Be patient with one another, even in tribulation.
  V. Be helpful to others through service and hospitality.

We have, then, spoken of two similar but slightly different types of expository sermons. Both take a passage of about a paragraph (or possibly a short chapter) in length. This passage is chosen because it has one central theme about which several significant points can be made.

Having selected either the fundamental or a secondary theme to build around, the preacher then identifies the important, useful points the passage makes about the theme and states those carefully as main points.

Let us consider a few closing comments on expository preaching. Expository sermons allow the preacher to dig deeply into the text and challenge him to uncover the meaning God has placed into the text and to make that meaning practical in the lives of his hearers. He will study the passage carefully in its context, word meanings, grammar, and applications.

A series of expository sermons through a book of the Bible can give a connected series that both provides good sermons and a residue of acquaintance with that book. Such a series, however, should move rather quickly and not seek to cover every verse in the book. It is important to be selective and to keep the focus on what messages can most benefit the audience. Such a series will, undoubtedly, lead the preacher to present useful lessons he might have overlooked had he not developed a series around a book of the Bible. This also allows him to treat sensitive subjects as they arise naturally and without appearing to have chosen them because some in the congregation especially need them.

The series approach, however, has some limitations. A congregation can tire of too many sermons from the same book and a preacher who limits himself to preaching only in such series may not find occasion to preach on some very needed subjects because they are not in the book he is preaching.

Also, a congregation needs some variety in approach to maintain their interest and if one preaches nothing but expository sermons, he may tire the audience of that type.

d. *Explained-Exemplified-Applied.* A fourth type of passage-based sermon is called Explained-Exemplified-Applied. Some teachers call this an expository sermon, but since it is not an analysis of a single passage, it is better to consider it a different type.

The Explained-Exemplified-Applied sermon takes as its subject sentence a verse or phrase from the Bible which presents some *principle* or *doctrine* and then examines that principle or doctrine under three main headings for the body of the sermon: (I) Explained, (II) Exemplified, and (III) Applied.

The verse, phrase, or word chosen as the subject sentence might, for example, urge the congregation to follow such a principle as "It is more blessed to give than to receive," or "Evil companions corrupt good morals" or "faith," "conscience," "courage," or other Bible concepts. In the *first* point of the body, the preacher *explains* this principle by definitions, elaborations, or clarification. Under the *second* heading, he gives "examples" *from the Bible* of this principle in action in people's lives. And in the *third* heading, the preacher "applies" the principle to circumstances in which the members of his audience may find themselves today. Here are some samples of Explained-Exemplified-Applied.

Subject Sentence: The love of money is a root of all evil.
Main Points of Body:
  I.   "The love of money is a root of all evil"—Explained.
  II. "The love of money is a root of all evil"—Exemplified. (Bible cases)
       A. Balaam illustrates this principle.
       B. Lot illustrates this principle.
       C. The rich farmer of Jesus' parable illustrates this principle.
       D. Judas illustrates this principle.
  III. "The love of money is a root of all evil"—Applied.

(Modern application)
- A. Remember this principle when you choose a job.
- B. Remember this principle when you have an opportunity to help others.
- C. Remember this principle when you give to the Lord.

Another example of this type of sermon is found in Jesus' Sermon on the Mount.

Subject Sentence: "Whosoever smiteth thee on thy right cheek, turn to him the other also."

Main Points of Body:
- I. "Turn the other cheek"—Explained.
  - A. What this principle means is . . .
  - B. What this principle does not mean is . . .
- II. "Turn the other cheek"—Exemplified.
  - A. Abraham's dealing with Lot illustrates this principle.
  - B. David's dealing with Saul illustrates this principle.
- III. "Turn the other cheek"—Applied.
  - A. When someone speaks unkindly to you, turn the other cheek.
  - B. When someone neglects you, turn the other cheek.
  - C. When someone treats you unfairly, turn the other cheek.

In developing this type of sermon it is important to remember that the second element must deal *only* with biblical examples because to introduce non-biblical elements there will leave confusion when the third element of "application" is introduced. Also, it should be noted that the application portion can be developed either through a list of various situations when the principle can be applied (which would have examples as subpoints) or by using modern case studies as the subpoints just as point II used biblical cases.

Summary. The passage-based sermons, then, always start with a particular passage in mind and develop that passage in some way. The *textual* sermon uses the actual wording of the verse or phrase to get the main points. The *expository* sermon analyzes a passage for a *theme* and develops *what the passage says about that theme*. The *Explained-Exemplified-Applied* sermon looks for a principle embodied in a passage and then *explains* it, gives biblical *examples* of the principle in action, and then *applies* the principle to everyday life.

Now let us turn from passage-based sermons to the other major type—*subject-based*.

2. *Subject-based Sermons*. *Subject-based sermons*, unlike those which are passage-based, do not begin with a single verse or passage in view; rather, they begin with a *topic* or *theme*. They may focus Scriptures from all parts of the Bible on one central message. The main headings in such a sermon do not, of course, come from analyzing a verse or passage, but rather from *analyzing the subject*. There are many forms which this analysis and the resulting major divisions may take, but the ten most common are listed below. A subject-based sermon should be no less biblical than a passage-based if it is truly focused on God's message to man on a particular topic or need.

a. *Narration With Application*. A very simple yet effective type of subject-based sermon is "Narration With Application" in which the preacher chooses *some Bible story as the subject* of his discourse and *relates the story in considerable detail*. The *narration* is then followed with *applications* of the lessons of the story to current problems. A preacher may, for example, tell the story of Elijah at Mt. Carmel, supplying the important historical, geographical, and cultural details along with the biblical narrative. Following this, he can make useful applications to practical living.

Subject Sentence: Elijah's confrontation with the prophets of Baal at Mt. Carmel contains great lessons for us.

Main Points of Body:

   I. Narration of the story of Elijah on Mt. Carmel.

  II. Application of the story of Elijah on Mt. Carmel.

       A. Elijah's faith to stand demonstrates how firmly we should stand for right in the face of strong forces against us.

B. Elijah's dependence upon prayer exhibits the ultimate power at the disposal of the Christian.

C. Elijah's sudden flight from Jezebel indicates that even the strongest among us is subject to weakness.

While the Bible is filled with stories which are suitable for such treatment, care should be taken to find narratives which have an emotional climax for interest and which have ample opportunity for applications to life situations today. The story of David's sin and Nathan's visit, the story of Esther, the conversion of Saul, and a host of others are excellent as the basis for such a sermon. Normally, the subject sentence will mention the story and, perhaps, a general theme of the lesson with the body having two points: (1) the narration and (2) the applications.

On other occasions, however, the balance will be better if the telling of a rather short story is made the introduction and the main points of the body are all applications of the story. Another way to develop a "Narration With Application" sermon is to develop the elements of the story so that as each part of the story is told, its direct application is given at that point in the lesson. Thus the preacher would tell part one of the story and give its application, part two of the story and give its application, etc.

This type of preaching is simple but since most every person, young and old, enjoys a good story, the "Narration With Application" sermon can be quite effective. The secret of good story telling, which is essential in this kind of preaching, lies in finding the proper balance between including sufficient specific details for interest and information while avoiding slow, ponderous movement. It is also helpful for the story to be told with a climax—like a good drama.

b. *Logical.* Another "pattern" along which the preacher may cut his subject sentence into main headings may be termed the "logical approach." This does not imply that other methods are illogical, but the "logical" pattern places particular emphasis upon logical relationships. Particularly good for the sermon to convince, the "logical" type of division usually gives *"reasons why."* A preacher might, for example, state as his proposition: "All Christians should study the Bible daily." His main headings would present the *reasons why* this thesis should be accepted. Another sample:

Subject Sentence: I'm glad to be a Christian because:
Main Points of Body:
    I.   Being a Christian gives me a reason for life.
   II.   Being a Christian gives me a guide for life.
  III.   Being a Christian gives me a hope for life hereafter.

In the "reasons why" type, the subject sentence ends with "because" and the headings are the "reasons why."

Another style of logical pattern is one in which each point is built upon the preceding one:

Main Points of Body:
    I.   If any man is in Christ, he is a new creature.
   II.   The first step in becoming this new creature is the new birth.
  III.   The next step in being this new creature is Christian growth.
  IV.   To make this growth possible, the Christian must keep the spiritual and the physical in proper balance in his thinking and living.
   V.   This balance can be achieved only when the Christian allows proper time in his life for the spiritual as well as the physical.
Subject Sentence: The Christian, then, should spend sufficient time every week in specific spiritual activity.

This type of sequence the logicians call "chain reasoning." Each link becomes a main point of the speech.

    c. *Parties Involved*. Sermons may often be built around those *persons or groups (called "parties")* involved in a given situation. One may, for instance, speak on "the love of God" and demonstrate with His *love* to Abraham, His *love* to the children of Israel, and His *love* to Christians. A preacher may also select certain key figures in some biblical, historical, or current episode around whom to build his sermon. The story of the curing of Naaman's leprosy, for example, might be built around the different persons involved in the story.

   I.   The maid remembered God.
   II. Elisha served God.
  III. Naaman obeyed God.
  IV. Gehazi left God.

A study of the crucifixion could be viewed from the standpoint of the parties involved: the Jewish leaders, the mob, the soldiers, the thieves, and Christ. The birth of Jesus, likewise, may be seen through the eyes of the shepherds, the wise men, the parents, and King Herod.

    d. *Time.* Still another method of developing the points for the body of the sermon is according to time or chronology. The most common division of this type is *"past, present*, and *future"* and variations of this approach. Simon the Sorcerer, for example, may be studied *before* his conversion, *at* his conversion, and *after* his conversion. The beginning of the church, likewise, may be seen in *prophecy* and *fulfillment*; and the life of a congregation, either in the first century or the twentieth, may be considered in its *past*, *present*, and *future*.

Other variations of the time pattern involve a sequence of historical dates or events. The life of Moses may be divided into three forty-year periods, and the life of David into his *childhood*, his *flight* from Saul, and his *kingship*. Similarly, the history of the exile may be partitioned into the *deportation* to Babylon, the events of the *captivity*, and the *return* from Babylon.

    e. *Space.* There are also occasions when a subject may be approached from a *geographical* perspective. One might divide a sermon on Jesus' last twenty-four hours into (1) the upper room, (2) the Garden of Gethsemane, (3) the home of the high priest, (4) the Hall of Pilate, (5) Golgotha, and (6) the new tomb. The growth of the church could be preached under the headings of "Jerusalem, Judea, Samaria, and the uttermost parts of the earth." This last would also be a textual sermon since those very headings come from Acts 1:8. This illustrates the point that there are times, although they are not common, when the same set of headings might be arrived at through more than one pattern.

Other examples of the "space" pattern would be Paul's ministry in *Ephesus*, *Philippi*, and *Corinth*, or Paul's imprisonment in *Jerusalem*, in *Caesarea*, and in *Rome*.

f. *Analysis*. Many topics fall into certain natural divisions. Government naturally involves the legislative, the judicial, and the executive, while strokes in tennis are forehand, backhand, and serve. Every topic or object has such natural divisions. Many religious topics, likewise, may be *analyzed into their natural parts*. A sermon on conscience, for example, could be developed like this:

Subject Sentence: The Bible teaches us of three states of the conscience.
Main Points of Body:
   I. A Pure Conscience
  II. A Weak Conscience
 III. A Defiled Conscience

One also may analyze a topic such as "How the Jerusalem Church Grew"—a working church, a praying church, a giving church, a unified church. Paul's statement that we must "overcome evil with good" may be analyzed into such headings as: overcome hate with love, overcome pride with humility, overcome idleness with service. The natural divisions for baptism are: (1) *who* should be baptized, (2) *why* should one be baptized, and (3) *how* should one be baptized.

The analysis type of subject-based sermon is a common one. Since almost every subject has its own unique elements, a preacher can develop an excellent and memorable message around these natural divisions.

g. *Biographical*. Many preachers like to take a biographical approach to a sermon by considering the life of some great

Bible character or historical figure. Such sermons are usually divided by either the great events or the great qualities of a person's life.

> *Subject Sentence*: Abraham was a man of great faith.
> *Main Points of Body*:
>   I.   Abraham first showed his faith by leaving Ur to go to a land which God would show him (Genesis 12).
> II.   Abraham also showed his faith in solving the trouble with Lot over the land (Genesis 13).
> III.   Abraham also showed faith in offering his son Isaac (Genesis 22).

A biographical sermon on Paul might point to the qualities which made him great: He could *admit* his mistakes; he *applied* himself diligently to whatever he was doing; and he *never violated* his conscience.

Biographical sermons are interesting because they deal with people, give the opportunity for variation, and often use familiar material. The audience can easily remember them because they associate the points with a person they know about.

h. *Analogy*. Some sermons are actually an *extended analogy or comparison*, and, of course, the Bible is replete with possibilities for such. Paul compares the exodus from Egypt and entry into the promised land to the Christian's exit from the bondage of sin, living in the wilderness, and finally crossing the Jordan into the promised land of heaven (1 Corinthians 10). Sermons can be built on the church as the body, the bride, the kingdom, or the family.

> *Subject Sentence*: The church is the family of God.
> *Main Points of Body*:
>   I.   God, the Father, is the head.
> II.   Christ, the Elder Brother, is our example.
> III.   We, as children, support each other.

Christian living is frequently compared with running, walking, fighting, laboring. In this type of sermon, the points of comparison become the main points of the sermon.

Subject Sentence: Paul compares the Christian life to running a race.
Main Points of Body:
  I. Runners must train.
  II. Runners must strive.
  III. Runners receive a prize.

i. *Problem-Solution*. Obviously, this type of sermon is built upon some problem, either theological or practical, and after various solutions are proposed, the best is usually determined. The commonly given "steps in solving a problem" are of some help in developing a sermon of this type, but should not be slavishly followed: the awareness of a problem, locating and defining the problem, exploring possible solutions to the problem, determining the best possible solution, securing acceptance for this solution.

In some cases, *the discussion of the problem will be the first major point in the body, the presentation of the solution the second*. In other cases the presentation of the problem will be handled in the introduction and the entire body will be given to examining the solution or solutions.

Some theological questions which might be handled in this fashion are: Which translation is best? Is salvation by faith only? What is the nature and work of the Holy Spirit? Was Christ raised from the dead? Practical problems would include: Should a Christian drink intoxicants? Can a Christian kill for his government? What does the Bible teach about divorce and remarriage?

j. *Motivated Sequence*. A number of speech teachers have devised specialized plans for developing a topic. Probably the best known of these is Professor Alan Monroe's "motivated sequence." Departing entirely from the usual introduction, body, and conclusion, he suggests five points for the entire speech: *attention, need, satisfaction, visualization, action*.

The first step in this plan is to center the attention of the audience upon the general theme to be presented; second, make the audience sense deeply a need or problem which demands action; third, show how this need can be satisfied through the speaker's proposed solution; fourth, make the audience visualize themselves with the solution in operation; and, finally, call for the action necessary for adoption.[1] This pattern starts by painting a dark picture of a need which makes the audience cry out for something to be done and then shows them the light as the solution is presented and visualized.

   I. Great Bible characters were often not good parents. (Attention)
  II. The results of failing as a parent are tragic. (Need)
 III. To succeed as parents we must use resources the Scriptures suggest. (Satisfaction)
  IV. Just imagine how you will enjoy seeing your children as faithful Christians. (Visualization)
   V. Now here are specific actions we parents should take now. (Action)

Summary. Here is how a preacher might use his knowledge of these various sermon patterns in developing a sermon. Suppose he has decided that a need in the congregation is for more home Bible study. So, he thinks through various possible sermon ideas: (a) a *textual* sermon on Deuteronomy 6:4-9 taking particular phrases about how the Israelites were to train their children; (b) a *textual* sermon on Ephesians 6:4 about fathers nurturing their children with (I) chastening and (II) admonition; an *Expository I* sermon on 1 Peter 1:22—2:5 about (I) God's Word is an incorruptible seed for a spiritual birth and (II) God's Word is spiritual milk for spiritual growth; a *passage-based* sermon on "nurturing" explained, "nurturing" exemplified, "nurturing" applied; a *subject-based* sermon (parties involved) on (I) Samuel's children, (II) Saul's children, (III) David's children.

Now with these possibilities in mind, the preacher can select

---

[1]Alan H. Monroe, *Principles and Types of Speech.* 3d ed. (New York: Scott, Foresman and Co., 1949), Chapter 16.

what he believes will best achieve his purpose with this particular audience and then proceed to other steps of developing the sermon.

Using the Main Points

It is unnecessary to try to place one type of sermon above another. Each has its own particular place of usefulness. Certainly no preacher will want to use one to the entire exclusion of another. There has, however, been a general neglect of good expository preaching and it should occupy a more prominent place in the work of most preachers. It has the advantage of keeping the Scriptures to the forefront while allowing many practical applications. A preacher must, however, learn to use all the sermon types well if he is to have success in the pulpit.

One last caution: It is very important to follow one and only one pattern at a time. If, for example, a preacher starts to develop sermon headings through the "parties involved" pattern, he must stay with it for all the main headings. Thus, the parable of the Good Samaritan might be preached through insights of the parties involved in the story: I. The Levite, II. The Priest, and III. The Samaritan. To add "IV. The Road to Jericho" would certainly confuse the audience.

Early in the sermon preparation process, then, a preacher should determine the main thrust of his lesson and express this in a "subject sentence." He should then "divide" this theme by a passage-based or subject-based pattern to provide main headings, worded in complete and parallel sentences, which follow consistently the same pattern. Such a skeleton for the sermon will give the audience a structure for grasping the message being delivered.

In some types of sermons, the *order* of the points is rather well established by the pattern itself. In other cases, however, special care must be given to *which points come first and last.* It is generally held by modern speech theorists that the strongest point should come first, and the next to the strongest point last, with the other points in the middle. If the audience is unfriendly to the proposition, the preacher may wish to save his subject sentence or proposition until the middle or end of the sermon, thus enabling him to begin with the point most likely to receive a favorable hearing. This technique allows the audience to begin in agreement with the speaker on the assumption that an initial agreement is more likely to produce final acceptance than an opening disagreement.

Much has been written of late about inductive preaching. In this style, the main point is not revealed until one has first worked through the evidence or information to be presented on that point. Such an approach can, indeed, create interest and give the audience a sense of greater participation. It does not fit every sermon situation but certainly should be considered for use when it is appropriate.

While no set of rules can be given to establish the order in which all points should be placed, the order in which the major divisions of the speech are arranged is important and should be given careful attention.

The *balance between points is also important.* While it is absurd to expect each division of the body to have an equal number of subpoints and occupy exactly the same amount of time, a proper balance should be sought. If any point is to be longer, it probably should be the first so the speech will seem to pick up speed rather than slow down. Nevertheless, no point should drastically outweigh the others, nor should any major point be so minor that it is actually inconsequential.

The total number of major points may vary from two to five depending on the nature of the subject, length of time, and type of outline used. As a general rule, the more main points, the less time which can be spent on each. More than five or six points is nearly always too many and usually results in a confused organization in the minds of the audience.

TRANSITIONS

If the points and supporting material of the sermon may be viewed as bricks, the mortar which holds the bricks together would be the *transitions* in the sermon. Some transitional statements are *rather formal*: "*Having seen* that Jesus fulfilled the Old Testament prophecies regarding the Messiah, *let us now look* to the testimony of His miracles." In this one sentence, the speaker both reviews the point he is concluding and previews the point he is beginning.

On other occasions, important transitions can be made by just a word or two: first, second, third, therefore, then, also, for example, moreover, likewise, in addition, consequently, another. Such words provide the glue which sticks the sermon together in the minds of the audience and helps them to get each part into its proper place as it is glued together.

Many sermons appear *well organized on paper, but to an audience they appear fuzzy and disjointed because the transitions are not adequate.* The nature of the sermon will, of course, dictate how obvious the transitions should be. If the sermon is to inform or convince, the audience should be fully aware of each point that is made and exactly when a new point is introduced. For this purpose the minister should employ such expressions as "having seen . . . , we turn to," and "next we must consider," and "the second reason for." He should take care to avoid overuse of the same transitions and such trite expressions as "we find that" and "we see that."

Sermons to stimulate and actuate, when geared more to an emotional than argumentative appeal, may not require such obvious transitions since the particular points being made are actually less important in achieving the overall response. In these sermons the preacher is not so interested in having the audience remember the main point as in establishing a mood and a response. Even in these cases, however, careful attention must be given to transitions, for whether they are made obvious to the audience, they must be included, and the subtle transitions often require more work than the obvious.

INTRODUCTIONS

While the introductory portion of the sermon may take no more than 5 to 10 per cent of the total time, it is a most important part. There is little point in arguing the merit of the adage "first impressions are lasting," for whether a speaker likes it or not, such is very likely to be the case. A good impression at the start will carry the audience far down the road to the desired response, but a poor beginning will puncture the tires before the trip begins.

In general an introduction should accomplish three objectives: (1) gain attention to the subject, (2) provide necessary background material, and *(3) gain the good will of the audience.* By the time the speaker leaves the introduction and moves to the subject sentence and body of the speech, all of these objectives should be accomplished. In many cases, of course, the preacher will already be known and liked by the audience and will, therefore, need to do little in particular to gain their good will. If he is unknown to them, however, he must recognize the need for accomplishing this objective. In some cases, considerable background will need to be given to orient the audience to the subject, but in other cases little will be required for them to understand what will follow. Gaining attention to the subject or making the audience feel a need to hear what follows will, however, occupy an important place in every good introduction. The preacher should, therefore, keep in mind that the goal is not merely to gain attention, but to gain attention to *the subject.* A speaker may gain attention to himself by crawling to the podium, blowing a bugle, or telling the latest joke, but none of these draws attention to the subject unless he is speaking on gymnastics, bugling, or contemporary humor.

The introduction, of course, is composed of basic units—statements and accompanying supporting material—just like other parts of the speech; but the units are chosen to accomplish the particular aims of the introduction. A preacher may, for example, begin with a narration to draw interest to his subject, quote a testimony from a favorite author of the audience to gain good will and heighten the interest, and then supply factual information for background material.

Nearly any of the types of supporting material discussed in Chapter 7 may be used in the introduction, but there are some special techniques that may be helpful, especially in securing attention to the subject.

1. Perhaps the most frequently used method for beginning a sermon is the quotation or reading of some "text" from the Bible. When the sermon is textual or expository, the passage being studied should certainly be read in the introduction,

unless it is too long, but it should not necessarily come first. In the case of the topical sermon, a Scripture may or may not be used to introduce the topic. The use of the "text" has the advantage of keeping the Scriptures foremost in the sermon and it is a simple matter for the preacher to find this material to use. If used, however, it must be read well or its impact is lost; and on some occasions it will be better to precede the "text" with some other material to stir the interest.

2. Another technique for the introduction may be termed the problem approach. While this method is especially useful in the problem-solution pattern of organization and in the "need" step of the motivated sequence, it can be used in almost any type of sermon organization. The preacher might, for example, begin with an apparent contradiction in the Scriptures such as Paul and James on salvation by faith, and then proceed with the solution to the problem or he might present a problem by using the statistical information on crime, alcohol, or drugs.

3. *A statement or demonstration of the importance of the topic* to the audience is especially good when done well. On some occasions the importance of the theme to the audience may be implied by a narration, statistics, testimony, or quotations; at other times a bold statement of the importance followed by some supporting testimony will be effective.

4. In order to make the sermon appear relevant to human problems from the very beginning, some preachers like to start with a reference to a current event. Billy Graham has made frequent use of this method and with telling effect. The current event may be one of national or international import, or it may be a local event of note; but if it is well told and has a direct bearing on the lesson to be presented, it can be especially effective.

5. On special occasions or when the preacher is a guest speaker, some reference to the occasion may provide an effective beginning. On such occasions as a baccalaureate service, dedication of a building, observance of a special achievement or anniversary, reference to the occasion is almost mandatory. Mention may also be made of the surroundings or some special accomplishment of the audience. A sincere compliment will

always gain good will.

6. Still another method for beginning the sermon is the reference to some preceding part of the program. Mention of a song or prayer, for instance, may provide an exceptionally good way to start a sermon, and this has the advantage of striking the familiar and appearing spontaneous.

CONCLUSIONS

Any college debater can testify to the importance of the last affirmative rebuttal, for it is in this closing speech that many a debate has been won. Just as the first impression often determines the *hearing* of the sermon, the last impression often determines the *doing* of the sermon. In a sermon to inform or convince, the conclusion will regularly include a summary of main points made. In sermons to stimulate or actuate, the conclusion will be the point of final appeal and should be particularly persuasive. So the two strategies most associated with conclusions are: *summary* and *appeal*.

Most any type of supporting material may be of use in the conclusion, but the *interesting narration*, *vivid description*, *startling fact*, or *striking testimony* will be of greatest value. On many occasions the preacher will wish to challenge his audience and may even insert his own personal intent to do what the sermon has asked. *The conclusion must, of course, make certain that the audience makes the proper application of the lesson to personal living. Without this, all else is of little use.*

In many cases, the strongest emotional appeal will be reserved for the conclusion in order to end on a high point. The closing sentence should be strong, not an inept "Thank you" or a mumbled apology for having spoken too long.

If the conclusion is to be a real high point, it must not be too long. Some sermons resemble certain musical compositions which seem to come to a half a dozen good stopping places, only to begin again. Once the audience senses that the preacher is bringing his lesson to a close, they will not continue to give their attention for a very long period of time. *A good rule to follow in the conclusion, then, is this: plan it carefully, make it strong, make it brief.*

THE CLIMAX

One of the most important but most neglected aspects of sermon organization is the matter of climax, from a Greek word meaning "ladder." Careful design and structure are characteristic of all art, and in this sense, preaching must be an art. Just as no good musical selection attempts to move from beginning to end on the same level of volume and same rate of speed, so a sermon must have its peaks and valleys. Some preachers seem to "mount the pulpit" on the dead run and keep the same pace until they "break the tape" at the end of the race. Others begin at a snail's pace and, likewise, maintain the same rate of progress throughout.

One of the qualities which distinguishes great preaching from average preaching is this very matter of *climax*. First, it should be noted that a sermon has *not one* but *many* high points, with all of them woven into a structure that constantly builds toward the *highest peak*. The interpreter of a poem should be able to tell exactly how each line of the poem fits into his pattern of building toward the major climax. The actor, likewise, should be able to indicate where every line in a given scene fits into the climax of the play. The same should be true of the preacher. He should structure his sermon so that *certain major statements stand out as peaks of intellectual climax*. Some items of supporting material will be in the valley and will serve as relief or falling action, and other supporting material will build toward the *emotional climax* of the sermon. This emotional climax will usually be in the early part of the conclusion and will most often be triggered by a story with strong emotional appeal.

Of course, the preacher's delivery, to be discussed in a later chapter, also plays a vital role in the development of climax. Usually the intellectual peak will precede somewhat the emotional high point but these often will both come near the end. There should be a slight "falling action" after the highest climax so the sermon has the sense of being "rounded out."

A FINAL WORD

As each aspect of sermon building comes into view, it seems

to be more important than any other. Actually, the major elements, like the links of a chain, are of equal importance, for without each of them, the others are ineffective. A sermon which is well organized but which has poor supporting material will fail, but a sermon with an excellent choice of subject and excellent material will fail if it is not properly structured. Like the erection of a building, the construction of a sermon has many phases, and the preacher must be expert in each of them.

ASSIGNMENT

Organizing Material and Using Sermon Plans

1. Find, in printed sources, five sermons with the complete text which demonstrate the patterns presented in this chapter. Make a brief outline of each of them to demonstrate how the major points and the subject sentence exemplify the pattern you name. The outline of each needs only the title, subject sentence, and main headings. Include in these five at least two passage-based and two subject-based. Each should be identified by the specific type it represents. Be sure to give the source of the material.

2. Turn in sermon briefs for *six weeks of preaching to a specific congregation.* Each of these sermons must have a title, purpose, subject sentence, and main headings. No more is required but you may make fuller outlines if you wish. Each of these sermons must also be identified by type: some type of passage-based or some type of subject-based. This assignment should begin with a brief restatement of the needs of the congregation as turned in with Chapter 4. Then present the sermons in the order in which they would be used—Sunday morning and Sunday night for six weeks. Use a good variety of types and try to fit each sermon to an identified need of the congregation. Also consider some variety in subject matter.

3. Use some chapter assigned by the teacher such as Acts 2, Philippians 2, Jude, Revelation 2, or Matthew 5 as a base for ten sermons. All four passage-based and any six different subject-

based types should be represented. Include only the purpose, subject sentence, and main headings of the body. Clearly label each as to the specific type it is. These should be prepared to be turned in, but selected ones will also be shown to the class for discussion of various sermon types.

7 | Using Sound, Interesting, Powerful Material

"Speak thou the things which befit the sound doctrine" — Titus 2:1

INTRODUCTION

Suppose a preacher should stand before his congregation, pause a moment as he surveys his audience, then speak exactly the following words:

> From Hebrews 5:11 through 6:12 we see the contrast between the Christian who has grown to maturity and the one who has become dwarfed:
> I. The mature Christian can teach others while the dwarf needs still to be taught.
> II. The mature Christian is experienced enough to feed on meat while the dwarf continues to need milk.
> III. The mature Christian is patient (diligent) while the dwarf is sluggish.
> IV. The mature Christian presses on to perfection

while the dwarf lays against the foundation.
V. The mature Christian can enjoy the fullness of
hope while the dwarf is likely to fall away.

Having thus spoken, the preacher calls for an invitation song.

While this expository analysis is certainly adequate, the
outline standing alone can hardly qualify as preaching. The
minister must put *flesh* on this *skeleton*. He must elaborate on
these major points to make their meaning *clear*, but even this is
not enough. Like an expert diamond salesman turns his precious gem to catch the light in the diamond's various facets, the
preacher must make each facet of his sermon sparkle with
appeal. With expert craftsmanship, he must shape or "cut" each
of his main ideas so that as he holds it up for mental viewing,
it appears both *interesting* and *vivid*. In some cases, moreover,
he must find the means to *convince* the audience that a point is
true and in other cases he must *motivate* them to do what he
asks.

Before a *statement* of fundamental importance can evoke the
desired response, then, something must accompany it which
will give it more force, more appeal, more vigor. If the main
point is pictured as a bullet to be fired into the mind, something
must propel it. If the main point is seen as a board to be attached
to the wall of the mind, something must hold it there. These
propelling forces, these nails, are called *supporting material*;
and each main statement with its related supporting material is
called a *basic unit*.[1] The entire speech, then, is composed of a
series of such units. The statement may be the subject sentence
and the main headings the support or the statement may be a
main heading with items that support it. Consider, for example,
the following *unit* made of a *statement* and its accompanying
support:

Statement: Jesus is the light of the world.
Supporting material:

---

[1] Donald C. Bryant and Karl R. Wallace, *Fundamentals of Public
Speaking*, 2d ed. (New York: Appleton-Century-Crofts, 1953), 42.

There is a little church on a lonely hillside where they have neither gas nor lamps, and yet on darkest nights they hold Divine service. Each worshiper, coming a great distance from village or moorland home, brings with him a taper and lights it from the one supplied and carried by the minister of the little church. The building is thronged, and the scene is said to be "most brilliant!" Let each one of our lives be but a little taper—lighted from the life of Christ, and carrying His flame—and we shall help to fill this great temple of human need and human sin with the light of the knowledge of the glory of God.[2]

Thus, the statement is propelled by the narration which supports it, and the two complement each other. The *statement* will have little force without the *supporting material*, and the *supporting material* will have no direction without the *statement*. Together they constitute a *basic unit*, a building block, and when many such blocks are placed together in the proper order, they make up the entire sermon.

Summarizing, then, a group of statements or assertions, even though they be the result of careful analysis, is not sufficient for a sermon. Each of these must be accompanied by supporting material which will make the point *clear, interesting, convincing, or moving*. And these four words suggest, of course, the four purposes of supporting material.

The ancient speech theorists considered the gathering and use of material under the heading of *invention* and thought of three types of persuasion which such materials could achieve: *logical, emotional, and ethical*.

Logical material was useful as evidence on which to draw conclusions by induction or deduction. *Emotional* material was necessary to inspire and actuate. Material which would build up the audience's acceptance of the speaker and make him more believable was considered the use of *ethical appeal*.

This chapter on supporting material will: (1) *specify the types*

---

[2]D. Thomas, *The Biblical Illustrator*, ed. Joseph S. Excell, St. John, vol. I (Grand Rapids: Baker Book House, 1953), 18.

of material which can be used to achieve clarity, interest, conviction, and motivation; (2) *suggest how such materials can best achieve these ends,* and (3) *describe how to locate these materials.*

TYPES OF SUPPORTING MATERIAL

Quotations

One of the most frequently used types of supporting material for sermons is *quotations,* or *testimony,* and the most common source of this material is, of course, the Bible. One sometimes hears the complaint that a sermon did not contain a single reference to the Scriptures. If preaching is to be the communication of *divine* truth by man to man, the Bible itself should be the primary source of supporting material.

There are, however, other sources for quotations: commentaries, theological works, prose and poetical literature, hymn books, anthologies of quotations, historical works, encyclopedias, the newspaper, and even fiction.

Quotations from any of these sources may be presented in three ways: the *full quotation,* a *paraphrase,* or merely a *reference* to the quotation or the author. The method used should be determined by the purpose to be achieved. If, for example, the preacher wants to give the impression that a host of authorities agree with a point he has stated, he may quote one or two in full followed by a reference to others who agree without giving the full quotation each time. In another case, he may wish to paraphrase or to select from the quotation the short phrase which contains the point he is making since to quote an entire sentence or verse may obscure the important words. In this case, of course, he must be careful to avoid misuse of the testimony and, while the complete context does not always have to be quoted, the preacher should be familiar with the context and make use of a phrase or a whole sentence in keeping with its intended meaning. To do otherwise is dishonest. Quotations often occur in this familiar pattern:

Statement: Isaiah pictures the Messiah as a suffering servant.
Support with quotation:

(1) "Surely he hath borne our griefs, and carried our sorrows, yet we did esteem him stricken, smitten of God, and afflicted" (Isaiah 53:4).

(2) Kyle M. Yates interprets Isaiah 53 as a picture of "the servant's destiny, career, suffering, submission, and reward."[3]

Factual Information

In almost every sermon the preacher will need to present factual data, figures or statistics, historical data, dates and geographical information, archaeological findings, scientific discoveries, or even current events. Factual information may be considered as falling into three categories: *single statements, statistics, and descriptions. Single statements* of fact might be dates or figures giving such facts as height, cost, or amount. *Statistics* go beyond single statements of fact to a means of summarizing factual information by averages, surveys, compilations, correlations, and the like. *Descriptions*, the third type, are a means of using factual information to help the audience visualize a place, event, or person.

Some examples of the use of factual information will demonstrate this method of support.

Statement: Solomon was immensely wealthy.
Support by factual information:

(1) Solomon's annual revenue in money is said to have amounted to approximately eighteen million dollars (cf. 1 Kings 10:14; 2 Chronicles 9:13).[4]

(2) When the Queen of Sheba visited Solomon, she gave him, besides other rich gifts, gold worth more than three million dollars (1 Kings 10:8-10).[5]

---

[3] Kyle M. Yates, *Preaching from the Prophets* (Nashville: Broadman Press, 1942), 102.

[4] George L. Robinson, "Historical and Scriptural Digest," *The Master Bible* (Indianapolis: J. Wesley Dickson & Co., 1947), 1345.

[5] Ibid., 1346.

Factual information is often regarded as uninteresting, and this is true of the reading of a lengthy financial statement or a genealogy. But when factual information is used in the form of *description*, it can be quite interesting. Notice how Lloyd Connel utilized a factual description to create interest:

Statement: "One of the saddest things in the world is to have a son or daughter who is afflicted physically or mentally."
Support by description:

> I know of a little girl in Tulsa who is an epileptic. Her father and mother are members of the church there for which I preached for a few years. This little girl was so pitiful to look upon. She was in a wheelchair; she was about nine or ten years of age; she wasn't alert as she ought to have been mentally; and one time in a twenty-four hour period this little girl had 134 seizures. I used to visit in that home occasionally. This father and mother had married when they were very young, only about seventeen or eighteen years of age. When this little girl was nine years old, they were still very, very young and I thought it was so pitiful for this young man and woman to have a little daughter of that disposition and to have to provide and care for her. My heart always went out in sympathy toward them, as it does to all parents whose sons or daughters may be afflicted in this way, and I am sure you feel the same way. . . .
>
> My friends, I mentioned a while ago that one of the saddest things in the world is to have a son or daughter who is afflicted physically or mentally. I now call your attention to something that is by far sadder. That is to have sons or daughters who are afflicted, not physically nor mentally, but who are afflicted spiritually. . . .[6]

---

[6]Lloyd Connel, *Christ in the Mountain and Other Sermons* (Oklahoma City: Telegram Book Co., 1960), 512-54.

Explanation

Although dependence upon it should be kept to a minimum, there are times when a preacher needs to explain. Since this is a less interesting type of support than most of the others, it should be used sparingly and only in connection with other types. In dealing with a doctrinal problem or the exegesis of a passage, however, the preacher will need to *expound* and *interpret*, both forms of explanation. Another way to explain is by using *definition*. Explanation may also involve *evaluations*, *restatement*, and *discussions* of *"why and how."*

Notice this example of explanation which includes definition and restatement:

Statement: "Thirdly, our Lord died on the cross to fulfill Old Testament predictions."

Support by explanation:

> Notice, I did not use the word "prophecy." I steered away from that word on purpose. The word "prophecy" does not necessarily mean to foretell. Most prophecy does not foretell. Sometimes a prophet did prophesy and foretell at the same time, but a man can prophesy without foretelling anything. To prophesy literally means to speak on behalf of another. When we use the word "prediction," there is no misunderstanding about it. Jesus died on the cross to fulfill Old Testament predictions.[7]

In the next example of explanation, the preacher is interpreting a passage of Scripture:

Statement: "In Psalm 16, David predicted that Christ was to be raised from the dead."

Support by explanation:

---

[7]Jimmy Allen, "To the Lifted Up Christ," *Abilene Christian College Annual Bible Lectures* (1965): 33.

"Thou will not leave my soul in Hades, neither will thou suffer thine holy one to see corruption," wrote David. When we die, our souls go to Hades. Hades literally means unseen. The body, of course, goes to the place for the dead; it was not left in Hades. His flesh did not see corruption. If the soul was not left in Hades and the flesh did not see corruption, that means there was to be a reuniting of the soul and the body. But, when the soul and body were reunited, there was a resurrection. So, David, a thousand years before our Lord's resurrection, predicted that such would take place.[8]

There is a great tendency to rely on too much explanation and most preachers would improve their sermons by reducing their explanation and increasing other forms of support.

Comparison

An interesting form of support, and one which often involves the use of other types such as facts or narration, is comparison. In this form two or more thoughts or objects are "laid along side" each other. Their similarities and *differences*, then, are noted.

Note how this sample of comparison provides clarity, interest, and force:

Statement: "God is faithful."
Support by comparison:

Thumb through a concordance and you will discover this to be a favorite theme of the Bible. The beautiful strain is heard over and over again in varied forms throughout. There are pieces of music in which some sweet air recurs repeatedly, now you hear it loud, now soft, now stirring in sonorous strains, now soothing in plaintive gentle tones; but it is still the same air. And the blessed thought of the

---

[8]Ibid., 35, 36.

faithfulness of God thus recurs throughout the Bible.[9]

Another sample shows how factual information is also used as the basis of comparison:

Statement: "Churches begun in these various nations should be self-perpetuating."
Support by comparison:

> This is in effect what Christ wants, for in His charge He instructed the taught to teach others what they had been taught and to instruct them to teach others.
>
> A few years back Dr. Hurley, President of Salem College, was faced with funding an unaccredited college. He invited others to join him in the formation of the "Council for the Advancement of Small Colleges," familiarly designated as CASC. Member colleges banded together to focus attention on the needs of small, unaccredited colleges. Each college officially committed itself to an active program designed to bring early acceptance in their regional accrediting association. When a member college is accredited it must drop out of CASC. The expressed ambition of the officers of CASC is to put themselves out of business.
>
> Why shouldn't the missionary attempt to so train the converts so that he will eventually work himself out of a job?[10]

Example

The example is a preacher's most powerful form of supporting material. By providing an instance, a case, a story, an illustration, the preacher can clarify, interest, prove, or motivate. And by the example, he can usually do all of these better

---

[9] James Lefan, "To Our Source of Help," *Abilene Christian College Annual Bible Lectures* (1965): 16, 17.

[10] Don Gardner, "To See Our Opportunities," *Abilene Christian College Annual Bible Lectures* (1965): 227.

than with any other form of support. Those who want to hold attention, stir enthusiasm, gain support, and inspire action must use examples to do it.

Examples may be presented in many forms. Sometimes an example is merely a brief reference to a person, place, or event which calls to the mind of the listener already familiar details. Thus, one may merely mention "compassion like Abraham Lincoln," "patience like Job," or "determination like George Washington." Such quick glimpses bring vivid pictures to our minds and can be powerful.

The most valuable form of an example, however, is the story—a narration of a case which demonstrates the point to be made. In telling such stories, a preacher has his most powerful form of support. These illustrations or examples in story form fall into three basic categories: (1) comparative example, (2) negative example, and (3) positive example. Let us look at how each of these can be used and then at a fourth way to use examples also.

1. *Comparative Examples*. In the comparative example, the preacher presents the story of something from a different field of endeavor that helps make the point. The comparative example, then, is a figurative analogy since it compares two things that are from different categories of activity and yet which have certain similarities. Notice these possibilities:

Statement: "Christians must sacrifice to save the world with the gospel."
Support by comparative example:

> In watching the 1984 Olympic Games, we were all impressed with the gymnasts and the great strength and control they had in their bodies. The U.S. men, who won a gold medal, were led by Bart Conners, who had devoted over a decade to preparation. He had endured several operations and spent many hours every day in practice. This is the sacrifice it took to gain a gold medal. How much more, even, we should sacrifice to gain the eternal crown of life.

Notice that the preacher compares athletics to Christian living—a case drawn from one field of endeavor to illustrate actions in another.

Statement: "We should be looking for those around us who are lost."

Support by comparative example:

> In August of 1984, a seven-year-old Oklahoma City girl named Jennifer Goss was in her back yard. As she looked across the fence into the swimming pool next door, she noticed a still, small form floating on top of the water. She jumped the fence and went closer to find ten-month-old Zachary Wells face down in the water. She waded out to where the water was almost over her head to retrieve the child, now purple from the lack of air. She pulled the small boy to the side and began to squeeze him in her arms. Water came out of his mouth and soon he began to breathe. Because she was alert to those around her, she saved a life.
>
> Around us each day are those souls floating on the tide of life—soon to perish. Like Jennifer, we must be watching, caring, and even risking to "snatch them from sin and the grave."

Again, a comparison—from saving a life to saving a soul. Alertness in one area is used to illustrate the need for alertness in another.

Statement: "Climbing closer to God requires our maximum effort."

Support by comparative example:

> The *National Geographic* of July, 1984, tells of the efforts of 13 climbers to conquer a 3500-foot sheer wall on the east face of Mt. Everest. Carrying supply packs weighing 30 pounds on their backs, the group worked for 28 days in terrible conditions to make the climb. They had to contend with falling rocks, fog, snow, ice, avalanches,

and temperatures far below freezing. They carried thousands of feet of rope, oxygen tanks, tents, engines to lift equipment, and even small rockets to propel ropes up the mountain. They had to sleep in small crevices in the rock, walk across two-foot wide ridges above 1500-foot sheer cliffs, and climb rock walls hanging by ropes suspended from pitons driven into cracks in the rock. Three on a different team fell to their deaths while climbing nearby and, in fact, they saw one of them fall.

Such courage, such daring, such suffering and pain, such strenuous effort—and all to meet the challenge of climbing a mountain. How much more should we work toward our goal of reaching heaven and taking others with us?

Notice two or three things that are important in using a comparative example: (1) the comparison must fit—it cannot be strained or obscure; (2) the story must be interesting, involving achievement, challenge, daring, accomplishment, effort, emotion; (3) the story should be told with details to make it vivid and striking.

2. *Negative Examples*. In the use of negative examples, the preacher selects the point to be made and finds cases of those who have had undesirable things happen to them because they did not do what he is recommending. Thus, he urges honesty and tells stories of those who got into difficulty because they lied; he asks for abstinence from liquor and tells stories of those who have had problems because they drank; he encourages purity and recounts cases of those whose lives have been marred by fornication and lasciviousness.

Negative examples can be used as strong tools. Often there are instances of famous people, well known to the audience, who can demonstrate some undesirable trait: Alexander the Great, Marilyn Monroe, Richard Nixon. Cases come before a preacher frequently that demonstrate family problems, job-related problems, church problems, moral problems, financial problems—all of which illustrate the opposite of how he proclaims that people should live. While confidences should never be violated or people in the congregation embarrassed, the preacher can use his experience to provide stories that graphically demonstrate the results of failing to follow God's plan.

Statement: "Faithfulness in marriage is God's way."
Support by negative example:

> Some years ago two people married—the husband was a Christian, the wife was not. They attended church regularly and after a time the wife was converted. Two lovely girls were born and all was going well. After a time, however, the husband began to seek recreation and excitement among those who were not Christians and, before long, became involved with another woman. Over a period of several months he was unfaithful to his wife and all efforts to encourage him to repent failed. Finally, the wife divorced him but she continued to come to church with the two girls.
>
> It was not many months, however, until the wife began to receive attention from a man who was not a member of the church. She became interested in him and, because of her husband's unfaithfulness, claimed the right to remarry. As efforts to discourage her marriage to one outside the church were being made, her husband began to realize that the life he had chosen was not truly satisfying and that he would be much better off to be back with his wife and children. He came to her and asked forgiveness and sought to restore the marriage. By this time, however, her relationship with the other man had become strong and she had no desire to take her husband back. So she married out of the church and never came back again. Her first husband was restored to Christ and has since been a faithful Christian, living alone.
>
> Think of the terrible price he has paid for his "fling." His wife out of duty, his children not brought up in the church, and he living a celibate life—all because he chose a few months of immoral living.

The story is true, the details are vivid, the emotion is strong, the impact is to the point.

Here is another instance of a negative example.

Statement: "Honesty is best."
Support by negative example:

> A student in college was having trouble with his grades but still wanted to be in many activities and have a good time. He decided he could meet all of his objectives— graduation and a good time—by cheating on examinations. After all, he thought, it really didn't matter whether he learned all those things or not. So he cheated and graduated. But he could not enjoy his college degree. The thought of presenting himself as something he was not and of reaping the benefits of what he had gained dishonestly plagued him. He could not get it off his mind. Eventually he mailed his college diploma back to the college with a letter of explanation that he must return the diploma because it had been obtained by deceit. What had seemed such a nice short-cut, but which was against the will of God, turned into a nightmare of agony and disgrace. God knows us and what is best for us. Each time we go against His teachings, we will "reap what we have sown."

3. *Positive Examples*. While both comparative and negative examples can be quite strong and useful, the very best supporting material is the positive example. In this case, the preacher tells of one who does exactly what he is urging his audience to do and of the good consequences it brings. When he urges faithfulness in marriage, he tells of those who have lived together after God's way; when he urges patience, he tells of those who have exercised it; when he asks for meaningful worship, he describes those who have achieved it; when he asks for lives of service, he tells of those who have demonstrated it; when he asks for courage in the face of death, he tells of those who have shown it; when he asks for enthusiasm in the spread of the gospel, he tells of those who have done it; when he asks

for maximum efforts in personal work, he recounts the stories of those who have demonstrated it.

Using positive examples, the preacher tells of those who are practicing exactly what he wants his audience to do. This type of example not only has all the inspirational possibilities of the other two types, but it also has the advantage of giving details of how a listener can do just what the preacher is urging him to do. It demonstrates not only that others have done it but how. From such stories, the audience can make the strongest application to their own lives. While one may be inspired by those who excel in athletics and may be impressed by those who have failed to do what they should have, these require a greater "leap" to application than do stories of those doing precisely what God wants. Also, the use of too many negative cases can be depressing, particularly if the examples are of failures in the church. Better to encourage by reciting successes.

Statement: "We should be looking for our own place in the service of God, pursuing it diligently."
Support by positive example:

> Leon Lugar was an executive with Phillips Petroleum Company when a stroke left him partially paralyzed. He could walk, but with a limp, and he could talk, but with slurred speech. The company gave him a disability retirement. Here he was with some limitations on what he could do but with many of his abilities remaining. How should he spend his time? How could he do something useful? Leon decided that with a lot of time and with a good knowledge of the Word of God, he should teach. He was not able to teach publicly very well but he could teach privately. And, after all, was that not where we had some of our greatest needs?
>
> So he made his decision. He would walk the streets of his neighborhood, knocking on doors, until he found someone who would talk with him about the Bible. Then he would seek to start a Bible class with them in their home. He would continue to teach them until they became

a Christian or until he felt he should spend time elsewhere. And so he did. As a result, this man with impaired abilities, but great determination and commitment, led many to the Lord. We likewise must find our place of service in the kingdom and fill it with courage and determination.

Statement: "We should look for our own place in the service of God and pursue it diligently."
Support by positive example:

> Rick Watson was in federal prison at El Reno, Oklahoma. A fellow-prisoner, Blake Williams, studied the Bible with him and taught him the gospel. What should Rick do? He was in prison, separated from his family, deprived of the freedoms which most others enjoy. What was his life now worth? What could he do? Could God really accept him? Could others accept him?
>
> He determined to give his life to Christ and to follow in whatever ways He would lead. Blake and Rick then converted others and led a congregation of faithful Christians inside the prison. Through their leadership and teaching, over two hundred prisoners were baptized into Christ in two years time. Rick edited a publication called the *Prison Exhorter* for free world brethren and through letters and phone calls, he kept several outside of the prison busy with correspondence courses, calls and letters to encourage, and actions to help families of prisoners. Eventually Rick converted his mother, wife, and children to the Lord.
>
> While Rick had certain limitations on his actions, he found a place to serve the Lord in an effective and powerful way. Let us find our place of service and fill it with equal zeal.

Statement: "Live for Christ to die in Christ."
Support by positive example:

> Facing death is one of the most difficult parts of living.

Yet, there are those who are able to prepare for that moment so well that they can face it with great courage and calm. Ira North was such a man. A preacher for the largest congregation of churches of Christ (Madison, Tennessee), he had often preached on how to live and how to die. Yet, at age 61, still very much in the prime of his career, he himself was stricken with cancer. Surgery and treatments and rest gave some hope, but before many months it was obvious that death was approaching. Ira did not despair. He had preached about a better life beyond and he believed it. So he made preparations for his funeral. It would be a joyous occasion, a time of celebration of a victory, not a moment of sorrow and defeat. He selected the speakers, the songs, and the order for the occasion. It would be called a "graduation" since he believed it was his time to move on to something better. He even asked one of the speakers to include in his comments an explanation of why, even though many had prayed for his recovery, he still had died. Ira did not want anyone's faith shaken by his death.

Because he was such a popular preacher and public figure in the Nashville area, 8,000 attended the funeral—many having to see and hear on closed circuit video. Just as he had hoped, it was an occasion of joy and hope. Of course there were tears from those who would miss him, but the spirit of optimism which he had projected so strongly in life was clearly evident even at his funeral.

Let us so live that we also can be prepared when death knocks for us. Let us have a faith which looks beyond this life and a hope which provides an anchor for the soul, both sure and steadfast.

4. *A Listing of Short Samples.* In addition to comparative, negative, and positive examples, there is also a fourth way in which to use examples effectively. In this case the preacher makes a list of situations in which the listener may apply a teaching he is giving. Suppose, as an instance of this type of example, a preacher has discussed being honest. Then he lists

in rather quick succession some of the circumstances of life where we are called on to be honest.

> So God calls upon us to be honest at all times. When we are trying to make an important sale, when we are applying for a job, when we are filling out our income tax forms, when we are taking a test, when we are answering our children, when we are trying to get or to get out of a date, when we are selling a house, or when we are explaining why a payment is late. At all times and in all situations God calls upon us for complete honesty—every time.

Accepted Truths

The final type of support is the use of an accepted principle of truth as support for a point the preacher wishes to make. In some instances, this truth will be accepted because it comes from the Scriptures. Other possible sources for accepted truths are "sayings," "proverbs," or statements established as true by experts or evidence. If such an accepted principle can be found which supports the statement a preacher wishes to prove, then he can tie what he wants people to believe to what they already have agreed to. A third source of such accepted truths is the process of generalization. By examining a number of cases, a preacher may be able to establish a truth which can then be applied to the statement which he seeks to establish.

To illustrate, let us suppose the preacher has a statement which says, "We should treat others with kindness even when they are unfair to us." As support he can use the accepted truth from Jesus that we should "turn the other cheek." He might also use such a commonly accepted saying as "you will reap what you sow." While that is also from the Bible, it is a generally accepted maxim in our culture. As an example of the third source, generalization, the preacher might relate several cases from which he generalizes to the conclusion that we can often reverse a downward spiral in human relationships by doing something good to one who mistreats us.

In a sermon titled "Led by a Little Child," Foy L. Smith applies a biblical principle of truth and uses several other means of support in the same paragraph:

> In Proverbs 22:6 we have the warning, "Train up a child in the way he should go; and when he is old, he will not depart from it." We cannot take too many pains with our children, planting in their hearts the way of righteousness, hoping that when they are old they will not depart from it. Many have departed from the way in which they were trained—Solomon did—but early training may be the means of recovering them. At least parents will have the comfort of having done the best they could. We are taught to believe that this admonition will become the child's second nature, and will never be obliterated. Childhood is the period in which life-impressions are received; let us, therefore, train him as he should go, not as he would go. We, as parents, should teach our children that going with regularity to the house of God is a divine injunction from heaven. Mothers who wait until little Johnny is five or six before he is initiated into church services are sinning against the church, themselves, and the little fellow. A young mother said to me not long ago, "I'm going to wait until he learns to be good before I take him." Yes, I have had to compete with that youngster and I want you to know that I will take the baby anytime! When you see a little man who sits up and behaves all during the service like a gentleman, you can put it down that he had early home training. It shows every time.[11]

In this sample, one not only finds application of an accepted truth announced in Proverbs 22:6, but also some explanation and an example.

FUNCTIONS OF SUPPORTING MATERIAL

With an understanding of these six types of supporting

---

[11] Foy L. Smith, *The World Is Yours and Other Sermons* (Oklahoma City: Telegram Book Co., 1959), 60, 61.

material, it is now possible to consider exactly how these may be used to clarify, interest, prove, and motivate.

Clarify

Basic to every attempt to communicate is clarity. Organization helps to make a presentation clear, but supporting material is also fundamental. Not only must the point be understood, it must be so clear that it cannot be misunderstood. The types of support most often used for clarification are explanation, example, and comparison.

Suppose the preacher wishes to make the point, "Worship must be in spirit and in truth." Basic to making this point "stick" is some supporting material to clarify. While worship is generally understood, the words "spirit" and "truth" as used here are not immediately clear. So he clarifies. First, explanation by definition: "Thayer defines spirit as the power by which a human being feels, thinks, wills, decides."[12] More explanation: "That is, God is a spirit, a spirit being, and man has a part of him which is like God. This is called his spirit, that part of him that thinks and wills and determines." Finally, he clarifies by contrast. "No longer, then, says Jesus, must man come to worship God at some particular place where the special presence of God is supposed to be. God, as a spirit, is everywhere; man, made in God's image, can commune with his maker at any time when he approaches Him through his spirit. Christian worship, then, is a spiritual experience and takes place when the spirit of man makes contact with God, who is spirit." The clarification continues through example: "Recall, for instance, the case of Paul and Silas. Although their bodies were held tight by stocks in a prison, their spirits, which could not be bound, soared up to be in contact with the Great Spirit through the medium of song and prayer."

By the various means of support, then, a speaker can clarify his ideas in the minds of the audience. He should use enough support to make the statement clear but not use unnecessary

---

[12]Joseph Henry Thayer, *A Greek-English Lexicon of the New Testament* (New York: American Book Co., 1889), 520.

time once the point is made.

Interest

In addition to clarifying, a speaker must also build and retain interest; otherwise, he will not be able to get even a hearing for his message, much less an acceptance. Since the *statements* which constitute the skeletal part of his message are not usually very interesting within themselves, the interest in the speech must be provided largely by the *supporting material* which he chooses.

But, someone may say, effective delivery is what adds interest to a sermon; and this, of course, is true to some extent. But a preacher must have something to say with his good inflection and must have words about which to gesture. Besides, interest cannot be long maintained by delivery alone, no matter how good it is.

Interest, as the term is used here, indicates that the speaker is *holding attention on his subject* and *creating a desire in the listeners to want to hear more.* He is making the hearer feel that *some need is going to be met.*

If supporting material is to be used to interest, then, it must meet two requisites: (1) *it must touch those motives or drives from which spring all human needs* and (2) *it must be presented in a form which captures the attention of the audience.*

The drives to be touched were listed in Chapter 4 on preaching to needs, and were explained in some detail there. They are also listed later in this chapter in the discussion on motivation. But if a preacher is to make a sermon interesting, it must touch those drives which make things interesting to us. I am naturally interested in what relates to my self-preservation, to my gaining social approval or affection, or to my getting and keeping possessions. As the preacher comes to each point to be made, he must ask, "How can I make this interesting to the audience? How does this point relate to the drives of individuals in the audience?"

Then the preacher asks the second question: "In what form can I present supporting material that will capture and hold attention?" Of the six types of support we have considered, examples in the form of narration are the most interesting. Descriptions and comparisons can also be good. Quotations are interesting only if they are short, from a source we highly respect, and have a striking connection with the point. Accepted truths are not very interesting and explanation is often boring— certainly if used without other types for very long.

To demonstrate, consider a sermon in which the preacher wishes to stimulate the congregation by relating the character- istics in men which make God angry. He might state, "God is angered by those who refuse to answer His call to service." Support for this point would come from the story of Moses at the burning bush when he made several excuses and finally asked the Lord to send someone else. Exodus 4:14 states, "And the anger of Jehovah was kindled against Moses." In using this situation for support of his point, the preacher would meet the qualifications given above, for the relation of the story would use both description and narration, and he would touch the drives of self-preservation and respect for God since to anger God would be contrary to both of these.

In another case, the preacher may wish to use interesting support for his point that "Honesty is better for us than dishon- esty." Interest can be built in this point by providing examples, perhaps in narrative form, of life situations in which honesty has been the best policy. For example, he may refer to the businessman who cheated the government in a deal for several thousand pounds of meat and who, upon fearing that he would be discovered, drove into the driveway of a funeral home and shot himself. This negative example, again, allows for narration and deals with the motives of self-preservation, social ap- proval, and convictions.

It is, then, primarily by supporting material that the speaker is able to maintain interest in his message; and without holding attention and creating a sense of need, he will not attain the desired response.

Prove
In sermons designed to inform, it will ordinarily be sufficient to interest and clarify; but when the goal goes past imparting

knowledge to persuasion, then it is necessary to prove the propositions presented in the speech.

As far as oral presentation is concerned, there are *two basic ways to prove*. One is through observation, that is, through the physical senses. You can prove that there are fifty persons in a room by counting them. Likewise, you can prove that helium is lighter than air by demonstrating to the sight that a helium-filled balloon will float upward when released in the air. Jesus used this method of observation when He showed Thomas the nail prints in His hands and when He told the disciples of John to observe the persons who had been healed.

Such observation provides factual information which becomes the basis of belief. This method of proof by observation needs to be appreciated by the preacher so he may understand its use in the Scriptures. The occasions for using this type of proof in the pulpit, however, are very rare. A scientist may demonstrate an observable phenomenon from his lecture platform, but the preacher will not often find the method of proving by actual observation to be useful in his preaching.

The second basic method for proof is reasoning, that is, *drawing conclusions through implication* rather than from observation. This is what Aristotle called logical appeal. Drawing conclusions through reasoning may be applied to three types of circumstances: (1) when we wish to establish as truth or fact something *which once was observable but which no longer is*, (2) w*hen we wish to make a decision about a principle or policy*, and (3) *when we wish to consider matters which lie in the "unseeable" realm of the spirit* and which are, therefore, neither matters of fact nor of judgment.

Let us clarify each of these. The Bible, in Isaiah 20:1, mentions a king named Sargon. Whether such a person ever lived is a question of fact. Until 1843 there were many who believed the Bible was wrong about this fact. In that year, however, an archaeologist named Botta discovered a palace near ancient Nineveh which contained the records of a king named Sargon. Sargon himself was no longer observable as a king, but his existence lies in the area of fact. We may reason from effect to cause that if there is a palace and a record of a king named Sargon, then such a king did live.

Now look at reasoning about human principles and policy. Some matters in the physical or human realm require conclusions that do not lie in observable phenomena. Observation, for example, does not allow one to conclude that a sunset is beautiful or that a movie is obscene. Some facts may, indeed, be found which will bear on these questions, but there is no way to put a sunset into a scale and weigh it and even if one could measure the wave lengths of all the colors, he would not have established its beauty. Whether a movie is obscene is a question which is not simply a matter of physical observation. Some reasoning must be applied through application of principles, comparisons, causes and effects. Other judgmental questions are: What is the best method for mission work in a given situation? What is the nature of God's providence? How is one justified by grace through faith? Such questions are answered by reasoning that comes from quoting experts on the subject, by applying an accepted truth to a new application, or by comparisons.

Now the third general area for reasoning deals with *spiritual realities*. Is there a supernatural, eternal being? Do I have a soul? Is there a heaven and a hell? These questions turn on reasoning about an "unseeable realm" which lends itself neither to physical observation nor to judgment on a matter of principle. We know that physical realities can be observed with the physical senses, but how do we "observe" spiritual realities?

Drawing conclusions about the existence of the "unseeable" begins with observations of physical phenomena. We can, for example, see the world we live in and know it exists. Next, we reason in the realm of policies and principles. A widely accepted premise is that "for every effect there is a cause." So, by this principle, nothing can exist without a first cause. But we still have not "proved" the existence of God. We have reasoned that certain facts and principles call for a next step but that step takes us beyond our finite world. Now we consider the *various alternatives*. One option is that matter has always existed and that it has acted upon itself to produce what we see. Another alternative, however, is that there is an intelligent, eternal, unseen, and unseeable power which has created and shaped our world. Neither of these alternatives can be established in the same way one establishes a fact, for we are dealing with the "unseen" realm. We can, nonetheless, reason about these alternatives. Which conclusion is more *consistent with what we have observed about matter? Which is more consistent with the principles that govern the "seeable" world?* Answers to these questions show us that accepting an eternal power who created by plan and intelligence is a more likely conclusion than that order came spontaneously out of chaos or that mind grew out of matter. Such options are totally beyond anything in our experience where accident and chance do not produce complex things or successful working objects. The more reasonable option, then, is that an intelligent, eternal being produced what we see. *The Scriptures tell us that the stronger our faith is, the more real the spiritual becomes to us (Hebrews 11); but this faith is not merely wishful thinking. It is, rather, based on all the fact and all the reasoning which we can apply to the "unseen" world.*

As we discuss the various aspects of reasoning, then, keep these three types of questions in mind: fact, principles or judgment, and spiritual.

There are four types of reasoning to conclusions which we shall treat here, and each is based on a type of supporting material discussed earlier. We may think of each of these types of reasoning *as a "form" or mold into which we can pour our supporting material so that it may harden into proof.* Our mind naturally accepts these types of reasoning as conclusive when they are strong enough and all of these are forms which we use commonly whether or not we are trained in reasoning. We can, however, learn to use them more effectively by studying them.

1. The first type of reasoning is *reasoning from authority.* Into this form we pour quotations in the nature of testimony, and it must be a sufficient amount of testimony from reliable sources so that it may harden into proof for the proposition. If one were attempting, for example, to establish the principle that "Jesus is the Christ," he might use reasoning from authority by quoting a host of those who have stated their belief that this

proposition is true. He could quote from Peter (Matthew 16:18), from John (John 20:31), Stephen (Acts 7:56), the centurion who crucified Him (Matthew 27:54), John the Baptist (John 1:29-34), and, finally, God Himself (Matthew 3:17). Additional strength could be gained by quoting men outside the Bible who have believed. When all this testimony is poured into the form we call "authority," it makes a strong proof. Its strength lies in the fact that much of this testimony comes from eyewitnesses who had no personal gain to receive from such testimony, and the transmission of their testimony has been closely guarded. These witnesses meet the usual tests applied to witnesses in a court of law and so are to be believed. To create belief, a testimony must be from a reliable source in a position to know that what he is saying is true. His testimony must be accurately transmitted, and the quotation must not be taken out of context.

Actually we are using *reasoning from authority* anytime we seek to prove by quoting from the Scriptures. If we are dealing with those who regard the Scriptures as authority, this is an excellent method of proof. If we are dealing with those who do not, then we must first come to an understanding about a common authority to which we can both turn. Reasoning from authority is a form of "generalization" because we usually take several authorities and, from these, we generalize to a conclusion. Reasoning from authority basically says, "I accept this as true because those whom I believe have said it is true."

2. A second method of proof by reasoning is *reasoning from example*. In this type, representative examples or instances are poured into the form. If the number of cases is sufficient and they are truly typical, not rare or contrived, then a strong column of support is made. This method, also called generalization or induction, is easily demonstrated by considering the proposition that "no act which God has declared a sin is in the ultimate best interest of either an individual or society." As proof for such a principle, one may call upon a great host of sins as instances in which the statement is seen to be true: murder, stealing, fornication, lying, envy, malice, drunkenness. Each of these cases will demonstrate that committing this act is not in the ultimate best interest of the one who does it nor of society

in general. Since the proposition is seen to be true in a large number of cases, and since no cases to the contrary may be found, the proposition is demonstrated as true.

In connection with reasoning by example it should be noted that in some situations *every possible case* may be examined while in other situations only a *limited number* are available for observation. In either case, a conclusion may be drawn, but it should be presented as a less certain conclusion when some samples remain unexamined. This type of reasoning says, "Since there are cases where this point is true and no cases where it is not, I am willing to accept this conclusion."

3. The third type of proof is *reasoning from analogy*, and the type of supporting material used in filling this "form" is comparison. On many occasions we observe striking similarities between two objects, events, or persons, but on one particular point of comparison we have information on only one of the two objects.

Reasoning from analogy leads us to conclude, however, that if the two items are similar in all or most of the known aspects, they will be similar in the unknown aspect. The most popular illustration of this type of reasoning is the story of the two ostriches on the desert. A traveler observed that the two birds had similar feet, legs, bodies, and necks, but one bird had his head in the sand. By analogy he concluded that the head he could not see was like the head he could see.

Reasoning from analogy is a common method for the social scientist and, thus, is often useful for the preacher. Many historians, for example, have observed that all of the great world civilizations have fallen to outside attack only when they were weakened from within by moral and spiritual decay. By analogy one can reason that as these signs appear in our own civilization, there is cause for concern and alarm. James used this type of argument when he said that Elijah, "a man of like passions with us," prayed and it did not rain for three years and six months. So if we are like Elijah in many respects, we too should be able to offer effectual prayers.

Special care must be taken to use *only literal and not figurative analogies* as a means of proof, for no argument can be made by comparing objects basically unlike. One may correctly argue, for example, that when Israel as a nation was faithful to God the nation prospered and, therefore, that when any nation is righteous, God will exalt it. In this case, a nation is compared with a nation. But one may not reason that since no arrow has more than one head, no church should have more than one preacher. Arrows and preachers are basically unlike and the comparison is figurative, not literal. Such comparisons are sometimes valuable for clarity or emphasis, but are unsuitable for proof. Of course, where the Scriptures have approved a figurative comparison or a "type-antitype" relationship, such may be used for proof. (See 1 Corinthians 10, for example.)

4. The fourth type of reasoning is *reasoning from accepted truth or application of principle*. This pattern of reaching conclusions, often called deduction, involves a series of statements or propositions which are related in such a way that a conclusion may be inferred from them. This type of reasoning is often syllogistic for any reasoning of this type is reducible to some form of a syllogism.

A special word about deductive reasoning may be worthwhile before its details are discussed. Such reasoning is extremely common in its informal dress. The housewife concludes that she will shop at Harp Brothers because their sales provide true savings. (All sales at Harp Brothers are good; this is a sale at Harp Brothers; so it will be good.) The child says, "It's not fair," when his brother receives more candy than he does. He reasons from the accepted truth that "all children in a family should be treated alike." The businessman says that now is a good time to buy stock because the trend lines look favorable. All of these are conclusions based on an accepted truth or a principle. The conclusions are no stronger than the basic premise upon which they are based, but often one needs some practice in recognizing premises in order to examine their validity. A preacher is not likely to use deductive reasoning in the formal dress in which we are now going to look at it. But this practice will help him to recognize the pattern of such reasoning and to use it more accurately when he does make such statements. For those who wish to study a different approach than the syllogistic, the Toulmin system will be of interest.[13]

Reasoning or drawing conclusions from accepted truths or principles obviously *starts with a statement which either requires no proof or which has already been established by some other form of proof.* Our minds are well stocked with such truths. Those statements with which all agree without proof might be termed axioms. Some examples of these would be: "a parent should love and care for his child"; "anything a weak man can lift, a strong man can lift"; "a preacher should be sincere." Jesus used this type of reasoning when He declared that "If ye, then, being evil, know how to give good gifts to your children, how much more shall your Father who is in heaven give good things to them that ask Him?" (Matthew 7:11). His accepted truth was, "Anything man can do, God can exceed."

Some statements may require proof by testimony, example, or analogy, but when they are thus proved, they then can become the basis for deduction.

Once the authority of the Bible is accepted, moreover, then any statement from it may be used as a truth from which to reason. Other situations for reasoning from principle include such areas as morals, home life, and church work. After citing some examples to establish the principle as true, for instance, a preacher might conclude that since most conversions today involve private contact, every congregation needs an active personal work program.

Now let us look briefly at the more formal structure of reasoning from premise. Since the syllogism has been devised as a means for showing deduction in its "barest" elements, we will use the syllogism to explain this "mold" for proof.

Categorical Syllogism. The first and most common type of syllogism is called "categorical." The name is appropriate because this type of reasoning involves a category and a quality which is true of every member of the category. The reasoning goes like this: (1) there is a category of objects called "X," (2) every object in that category has the quality of "Y," (3) since

---

[13]See Douglas Ehninger and Wayne Brockriede, *Decision by Debate* (New York: Dodd, Mead & Co., 1963), 98-189.

"Z" is an object in the category of "X," "Z" has the quality of "Y."

Notice how this pattern is applied in the following syllogism:

> *Major premise*: All men (category X)
>   are mortal (quality Y).
> *Minor premise*: Socrates (object Z)
>   is a man (category X).
> *Conclusion*:   Therefore, Socrates (object Z)
>   is mortal (quality Y).

In symbolic terms, we may express the categorical syllogism like this with ">" meaning "is included in."

> All X>Y (all X is included in those with quality Y)
>   Z>X (all Z is included in X)
> Therefore Z>Y (all Z is included in those who have
>   quality Y)

In the form of the categorical syllogism we are studying, the terms of the syllogism always come in this order:

> *Major premise*: major term (X)—middle term (Y)
> *Minor premise*: minor term (Z)—major term (X)
> *Conclusion*:   minor term (Z)—middle term (Y)

Remember, the *major* term is the name of the *category*; the *middle* term is going to be the *linking element* as the *characteristic* of the major term. The *minor* term is the name of the *specific entity* which, if the syllogism is correct, will have the quality that all in the major term have. *Only when the order is precisely after this pattern is the syllogism considered valid.*

Of what practical value is this to the preacher? Undoubtedly, every minister will find himself doing this type of reasoning, and he should be aware of what he is doing and whether it is actually valid. The preacher may say, for instance, "Jesus declared that the pure in heart shall see God; so if you want to see God, you must be pure in heart." Such a statement is a categorical syllogism in informal dress. More formally, it might be stated:

> *Major Premise*: "The pure in heart (X) shall see God (Y)"
> *Minor Premise*: You (Z) are pure in heart (X).
> *Conclusion*:   Therefore, you (Z) shall see God (Y).

The preacher will also want to use such reasoning for proof of his statements. In nearly every such case, his major premise will be a statement of Scripture.

> *Major Premise*: "All that would live godly (X) shall suffer persecution" (Y).
> *Minor Premise*: I (Z) am living godly (X).
> *Conclusion*:   Therefore, I (Z) will suffer persecution (Y).

> *Major Premise*: "All that believe and are baptized (X) will be saved" (Y).
> *Minor Premise*: I (Z) have believed and been baptized (X)
> *Conclusion*:   I (Z) will be saved (Y).

Notice that in each case, the major premise first *names the category* and *then gives the characteristic*; the minor premise *names the specific object* and *places it in the category*; and the conclusion *restates the specific object* and *attributes to it the quality* which belongs to all in the category. This order is very important and should be followed in every case until one has studied the matter very carefully in more detailed works where other patterns can be learned. Notice, too, that before a certain conclusion can be drawn, the quality must be ascribed to "all" in the category. If it can only be said that "some" who start to drink become alcoholics, then one cannot conclude that any one particular person who starts to drink will become an alcoholic. He can, however, reason as follows:

> *Major Premise*: Only those who start to drink become alcoholics.
> *Minor Premise*: I have not started to drink.
> *Conclusion*:   Therefore, I will not become an alcoholic.

Since one of the above premises is negative, the conclusion must be negative. If both premises were negative, no conclusion could be drawn.

Special care must be taken not to fall into the trap of the illicit minor, as the logicians call it. That is, one must be certain that the minor premise actually places the person in the category under consideration. The following syllogism looks good at first, but is it?

> *Major Premise*: All humanists (X) believe that there is no God (Y).
> *Minor Premise*: Smith (Z) believes that there is no God (Y).
> *Conclusion*:   Therefore, Smith (Z) is a humanist (X).

Instead of placing Smith in the category of humanists, however, the minor premise attributes to him the quality of those in the category. Notice how the order of terms has been altered to X-Y, Z-Y, Z-X. This varies from the one given above and is a clue that the conclusion does not follow. The major premise does not say that only humanists believe there is no God, for such is not the case. The minor premise is, therefore, said to be illicit, for it fails to do its proper job of placing the object into the category. The reasoning in the above example, then, is fallacious.

While preachers will not often use a full, categorical syllogism in a sermon, they will often use it in a shorter or less formal wording. "Since the Bible says all liars shall suffer eternal punishment (Revelation 21:8), we must be very careful to tell the truth." "Since Jesus says it is wrong to lust, I should not look at obscene pictures." Put in its more formal wording, this last one would read:

> *Major premise*: All who lust are sinning.
> *Minor premise*: Looking at obscene pictures will make me lust.
> *Conclusion*: Looking at obscene pictures is sinning.

The categorical syllogism, however, is not the only form of the syllogism. There are two others which should be mentioned briefly: *the hypothetical and the disjunctive*. While the names sound foreboding, they are not difficult to grasp.

Hypothetical Syllogism. The hypothetical syllogism is built on an "if" statement, hence the name hypothetical. The major premise in this case is composed of two clauses, named the *antecedent* and the *consequent*. It states that should the antecedent or "if" part come true, then the consequent will follow. The minor premise, then, indicates that the "if" clause either has or has not come to pass, and the conclusion then affirms or denies the consequent.

If we let "⊃" read "if-then," we may diagram the hypothetical syllogism like this:

$$A \supset B \quad \text{If "A" then "B"}$$
$$\underline{A} \qquad \text{"A" is true}$$
$$B \qquad \text{therefore, "B" is true}$$

If the antecedent is denied, the form goes this way:

$$A \supset B \quad \text{If "A" then "B"}$$
$$\underline{A'} \qquad \text{"A" is not true}$$
$$B' \qquad \text{therefore, "B" is not yet established}$$
$$\qquad \text{but could be true}$$

Another valid form of the hypothetical syllogism is:

$$A \supset B \quad \text{If "A" then "B"}$$
$$\underline{B'} \qquad \text{"B" is not true}$$
$$A' \qquad \text{"A" is not true}$$

If salvation is by election (A) then God must be a respecter of persons. (B) God is not a respecter of persons (B); therefore, salvation is not by election (A).

An even stronger form is "if and only if." This is symbolized by "≡" but can be used only if such is actually true.

$$A \equiv B \quad A \equiv B \quad A \text{ "if and only if" } B$$

$$\frac{A}{B} \quad \text{or} \quad \frac{A'}{B'} \qquad (B \text{ cannot be true})$$

Here are some examples:

> *Major Premise*: If (and only if) Jones passes history (A) then he will be eligible for football (B).
> *Minor Premise*: Jones passed history (A).
> *Conclusion*:   Therefore, Jones will be eligible for football (B).

or

> *Major Premise*: If (and only if) Jones passes history, (A)
> *Minor Premise*: Jones did not pass history (A′).
> *Conclusion*:   Jones will not be eligible for football (B′).

The hypothetical syllogism was a favorite logical form of Jesus. In Matthew 22:29-31, for example, Jesus reasons that if God (in Exodus 3:6) could refer to Himself as currently the God of Abraham, Isaac, and Jacob (present tense of the verb) long after they had died, then they must still be alive in some sense after they were dead. God did so refer to them. Therefore, they must still be alive in some sense.

In Luke 15:13 and 14:6 Jesus reasoned: if it is proper to care for animals who need assistance on the Sabbath Day, then it would be proper to care for humans who need assistance on the Sabbath Day. It is proper to so care for animals (the ox out of the ditch). So it is proper to care for humans in need on the Sabbath.

Another case of Jesus' use of a hypothetical syllogism is in Matthew 6:30: "If God doth so clothe the grass of the field, shall he not much more clothe you." Implicit is the conclusion that God does care for the grass and will care for humans.

Paul, likewise, used hypothetical syllogisms. First Corinthians 15, for example, is filled with such reasoning.

> *Major premise*: If Christ is not risen (A), then your faith is vain (B).
> *Minor Premise*: You know your faith is not vain (B´).
> *Conclusion*: Therefore, Christ is risen (A´).

John 20:31, likewise, is a statement which suggests that we should use a hypothetical syllogism: "Many other signs therefore did Jesus in the presence of his disciples, which are not written in this book; but these are written that ye might believe that Jesus is the Christ." In formal wording, this hypothetical syllogism goes like this:

> *Major premise*: If one can do signs that can only be explained by divine power, then his claims are to be believed.
> *Minor Premise*: Jesus, who claimed to be the Christ, could do such signs.
> *Conclusion*: Therefore, Jesus' claims to be the Christ are to be believed.

The preacher will find many occasions for using the hypothetical syllogism in brief form: "If we can raise the contribution $50 a week, we can send another missionary to Africa"; "If we can organize the Bible classes more effectively, we can increase the attendance."

Not only will understanding different forms of reasoning help one to present such reasoning himself, but it will also help him interpret the Scriptures as well.

Disjunctive Syllogism. The final type of reasoning from premise or generalization is the disjunctive syllogism, an "either-or" statement. In this case the major premise states two alternatives, either of which is possible. If the reasoning is to be valid, however, it must be impossible for both to take place. The minor premise, then, either accepts or rejects one alternative; and the conclusion, then, accepts or rejects the other.

The disjunctive syllogism may also be represented symbolically with "⩑" reading "either . . . or . . . but not both."

       C ⩑ D   Either "C" or "D" but not both
          C   "C" is true
          D   therefore "D" is not true

The preacher might use this form of the syllogism in this way:

> *Major Premise*: Either Christ is the Son of God (C) or
>   He was an imposter (D).
> *Minor Premise*: He was not an imposter (D).
> *Conclusion*:   Therefore, he was the Son of God (C).

Special care must be taken to see that it is not possible for both alternatives to occur.

> *Major Premise*: Either we can build a new building (C)
>   or we can send more missionaries to
>   other places (D).
> *Minor Premise*: We should build a new building (C).
> *Conclusion*:   Therefore, we cannot send any more
>   missionaries to other places (D).

This may look plausible on the surface and may in some cases be valid, but it might be possible to do both and the decision to do one would not, then, necessarily rule out the other.

In Mark 11:31, 32, Jesus used a disjunctive syllogism with the Jewish leaders. He asked them, "Was John's preaching from heaven or from men?" He gave them two alternatives, both of which could not be true. Unfortunately for them, they did not want to accept either alternative. If they said, "from men," they would be in trouble with the people; but if they said, "from heaven," Jesus would ask why they had not gone out to Him.

5. A special word should be said in this section on reasoning about *causal relationships*. In many discussions of reasoning, *reasoning from cause* is listed as a separate type, and, indeed, it may be so considered. Yet, reasoning about causes and effects actually involves the use of generalizations from cases and deductions from accepted principles. For this reason, it is not considered as a separate type of reasoning in this study. Since many discussions of religion do involve causal relationship, however, a few comments on it will be useful.

All accept the principle that "nothing happens without a cause." Thus, for every occurrence, something happened to bring it about. The event out of which other events occur is called the *cause* and the resulting events are called effects. It is often very useful to discover what caused an event to happen. Since it is accepted that there is no effect without a cause, one looks to find a prior event without which the effect could not have happened. *A cause, then, may be defined as the indispensable antecedent of the effect.*

Jesus recognized this principle when He advanced the precept, "By their fruits ye shall know them" (Matthew 7:16). A fruit, obviously, is an effect; and when we reason that since a program's fruits are "good," the plan which caused them is "good," we have used causal reasoning based upon the application of an accepted principle (deduction).

The strength of reasoning from cause lies in establishing the certainty of the relationship between the cause and the effect. Usually the effect is known and the search is for the cause. The contribution has taken a sudden increase and has maintained the larger amount over several months, so the effect is clear. But what was the cause? Investigation reveals that the only change in the previous system was the presentation of an expanded program and an appeal for increased support. The conclusion, then, is drawn that this presentation and appeal caused the larger offering.

Reasoning about causes has played a large part in discussions of Christian evidences. Arguments for the resurrection of Jesus have often been built on a causal foundation. Take, for example, the change in Peter from his denials to his preaching on Pentecost. Some event must be found which produced such an astounding change, and that event, it is argued, was the Resurrection. No other cause, the reasoning goes, could have produced this effect for no lesser cause could have produced a change of such magnitude.

Another causal argument relating to the resurrection is the one which says that while the resurrection may be very difficult to explain, the early development of Christianity is even harder to explain without it. This argument, of course, moves from effect to cause, and is based on a principle which says that some event of striking significance must have occurred following the death of Jesus to bind His followers together and to stir them to their zealous proclamation of the gospel. Nothing short of seeing the resurrected Lord provides a cause sufficient to produce this effect.

Causal relationships also occupy an important place in discussions regarding the existence of God. Since all agree that the world as it now exists had to come from somewhere, there have been voluminous discussions attempting to establish the cause for the now existing effect. Materialists and atheists argue that everything here now has come from non-living matter through millions of years of evolution. Believers in God, on the other hand, argue that God Himself is the "first cause," and that it is far more reasonable to accept "mind" as the designer and originator of the cosmos than to believe the universe came from unexplained, nebulous matter, making the present arrangement an accumulated accident. Causal reasoning may be set up according to various syllogisms:

> Either the universe came from mind or matter. It could not have come from matter (insufficient cause); therefore, it must have come from mind.

> or

> Either the early church gave up their lives for a Savior they knew had failed and was a liar or they had reason to

believe He was truly risen. They would not give their lives
for a lie, therefore, they had reason to believe He was risen.

A preacher, then, must be able to use supporting material to
prove. He does this by utilizing one of the four processes of
reasoning: (1) from testimony by using quotations or reference
to accepted authorities, (2) from typical cases by presenting
sufficient instances or examples, (3) from analogy by comparing two like objects, and (4) from premise by applying an
accepted truth or principle to the particular case at hand.

Motivate

Finally, supporting material provides the basis for motivation, the most demanding part of preaching. To inform or
convince is not too difficult, but moving an audience to feeling
and action is.

It is not possible, of course, to separate completely "logical,"
"ethical," and "emotional" appeals. One sentence could em-
body them all and no persuasion or motivation is complete
unless all three are involved. Since, however, we have discussed ethical appeal in the discussion of the preacher's character and logical appeal in an earlier part of this chapter, we
shall now consider emotional appeal and how it may be used to
motivate.

Use of emotions in preaching is an important but delicate
matter. No preacher can succeed without using the potential for
good in the emotions of his audience, but the possibility for
abuse of emotions is great. As we study motivation and how
emotional appeal can contribute to it, we will first consider *how*
to motivate and then *to what degree it is appropriate* to use such
motivation.

Emotional appeal involves three basic areas: (1) the *message*
the preacher speaks, (2) the *words* he uses to say it, and (3) the
non-verbal cues in voice and body he uses while speaking it.

First, a preacher can motivate through the content of what he
says. He can say something to get an audience to feel and to act.

Basically, a preacher can move a listener when he can relate
what he wants them to feel and do to one or more of their basic

motives or drives. The ten fundamental drives were explained in Chapter 4, but must be given additional attention here since they all play such an important role in motivation.

A motive or drive is a fundamental, God-given need which exists in all human beings, and while countless lists of these have been compiled, for the purposes of this study, ten have been given: self-preservation, sex, social approval, possessions, affections, power, exploration, convictions, pleasure, and respect and worship. Our emotions, such as fear, love, hate, anger, disappointment, sorrow, and joy, cluster around each of these drives, since it is, in reality, about each of these drives that we feel the emotions.

The following list itemizes these ten drives and provides after each some statements a person might make who is fulfilling that drive. To motivate, the preacher must tie what he seeks for his listeners to do with their being able to feel the sentiments expressed in these statements. When they believe that doing what he desires will enable them to say one of the statements below, then they are likely to do what he desires. In each statement, let "X" stand for what the preacher wants the audience to do.

1. Self-Preservation
   a. X will prolong my life.
   b. X will fill a biological need for food or drink.
   c. X will keep me from harm or make me safer.
   d. X will increase my self-respect.
2. Social Approval
   a. X will give me recognition or respect from others.
   b. X will give me someone's good will or approval.
3. Sex
   a. X will give me physical sexual satisfaction.
   b. X will give me an emotional satisfaction as a man or woman.
   c. X will make me more attractive to one of the opposite sex.
   d. X will teach me something about satisfying my sexual desire.

4. Possessions
    a. X will give me money or its equal.
    b. X will get something for me or preserve ownership of something.

5. Pleasure
    a. X will give me physical comfort or enjoyment.
    b. X will give me mental enjoyment.
    c. X will help me avoid pain.

6. Power
    a. X will give me influence over someone or get them to do what I want them to do.
    b. X will allow me to exercise freedom of choice.
    c. X will help me do something most people can't or don't do.

7. Affections
    a. X will get me love from someone.
    b. X will help me give love to someone.
    c. X will help me receive acceptance from those I love.

8. Convictions
    a. X will help me do what is important to me.
    b. X will help me do my duty.
    c. X will enable me to live up to my code of ethics.
    d. X will help me understand my principles of conduct more clearly.
    e. X will enable me to do something useful to my community or country.

9. Exploration
    a. X will help me learn something new.
    b. X will help me meet a challenge.
    c. X will give me an adventure.

10. Respect and Worship
    a. X will give me a relationship with someone greater than me.
    b. X will give me a relationship with something greater than man.
    c. X will help me understand more clearly the power of the supernatural.

But how does the preacher relate his hopes of what the audience will do to those "springs of response" we have just reviewed? He can, of course, simply tell of this relationship. "If you want to preserve yourself," he might say, "then don't go to hell. Salvation will be yours." Sometimes such a direct appeal has value, but in many cases it will be through some type of supporting material, usually a narration, or a description, or a testimony, that a speaker can most effectively put his appeal to the listeners. Below are some of the especially effective ways to tie what you want a listener to do with his own desires.

1. *Tell a story that involves children, the elderly, or the handicapped.* Everyone seems touched by such narrations because we easily identify with them and have a natural affection for such persons. So the preacher tells of a blind teacher who used his faith to overcome a handicap as a way to motivate his audience to overcome their problems.

2. *Describe or tell a narration about persons who faced a difficult challenge and overcame.* We are attracted to books, movies, TV programs, and persons who have faced problems or hardship and have overcome through their drive of exploration and convictions and respect. What American, for example, was not moved when those Americans held by the North Vietnamese were released from their prisons and came out speaking patriotic statements and saluting the flag? They had overcome. So did early Christians, a high school senior who refused to take a drink when pressured by friends, and the businessman who rejected a dishonest deal to become a success. Telling these stories about people *who have done what you want the audience to do* will help to motivate them to action.

3. *Describe events or persons which will cause the listener to recall touching moments in their own lives*—the birth of a child, the loss of a loved one, the love for a pet, a wedding, a graduation, a moment of joy or sorrow. Such events are easily related to our drives for affection, pleasure, exploration, power, and sex. So, a reference to a mother sacrificing for her children will bring to mind tender moments for mothers and for children and for husbands.

4. *Give personal testimony*—either yours or another's—

which ties your objective to the listener's needs. If you and others have tried the attitude or action you are urging and have found it profitable, then this personal experience can be moving. Of course, testimony of those who have not done what is being suggested and are sorry can also be used.

5. *Help the listener visualize himself doing what you urge* and finding a way to satisfy his needs. In order to move a listener, a speaker should engage the imagination of the listener and visualization is an excellent way to do it.

Remember, as suggested in the earlier section on examples, you can give comparative examples, negative examples, or positive examples. All can be good for motivation, especially when they use content such as that just described. *The most effective, however, is the positive example, a story of someone doing what you want the audience to do.*

Having seen (1) the message or content the preacher may use to develop emotional appeal, we should also look at two other elements which are also important in achieving this end: (2) the words which the speaker chooses to convey his message and (3) the non-verbal cues of voice and body. While the main discussion of these aspects of preaching comes in Chapter 8 and 9, a few brief comments will be appropriate here.

Words not only have a dictionary meaning, but also they have emotional connotations which the preacher should recognize and use. Words with an obvious emotional coloring are such terms as "lost," "racist," "mother," "failure," "victory," "heaven," "hell," "hate." Notice the difference in the emotional tug of the two following sentences, both of which have basically the same content:

(1) "Those who do not tell the truth should expect to have some bad consequences."
(2) "Every liar shall spend an eternity in the torments of hell, eternally separated from the face of God."

To make his message moving, then, the preacher should choose the best words for emotional impact. In addition to content and wording, delivery is also a fundamental part of emotional appeal. How one accompanies his words with the non-verbal cues of voice and body is very important in making listeners feel and act.

If, for example, the speaker himself is moved by a thought so that he cries or smiles or appears very earnest, then the audience will be more likely to show emotion. Preaching is not a game, of course, and the preacher should not stoop to tricks. He can, however, use material that is meaningful to himself and be open to responding to its force. Certainly his enthusiasm or sorrow or devotion to a cause will tend to create the same feelings in others. Some persons seem to have, by nature, a certain transparency of spirit that readily moves audiences. Others have to give more attention to developing this capacity. All, however, can improve on emotional impact of their delivery.

Now a few examples of emotional appeal which illustrate the principles just suggested. Jimmy Allen used these testimonies to stir an audience to accept Christ's power over death in their lives:

> T. B. Larimore, a few hours before his death, wrote: "My faith has never been stronger; my hope has never been brighter... my heart has never been calmer... I sleep soundly, dream sweetly, and rejoice evermore." Why should a man fear death if he has the title deeds of heaven in his pocket? John Banister told me of the death of a Christian friend. He said about ten minutes before the brother died, he gave a "V" for victory sign and pointed up. You can't beat that! The savior provided peace for him even in the hour of death.[14]

In this sample we see the appeal to power over death which all would like to have.

Another sample comes from Reuel Lemmons who used affection for mother and respect for Christ to appeal for his audience to reject sin and accept Christ.

---

[14]Jimmy Allen, "Christ, the Prince of Peace," *Great Sermons of 1967* (Austin: R. B. Sweet Publishing Co., 1967), 26.

It would be unthinkable that a youth should turn in ingratitude—inspired rebellion against a loving mother. Yet we rebel against a God whose love for us is greater than the love of a mother. We can hardly find words to describe our loathing for a man who will become a traitor to his own country—his own beloved land. Yet, we seldom feel repulsion at one who has become traitor to a heavenly Father and who has done despite to the spirit of Grace. When one treads underfoot the blood of the covenant by which he was sanctified, when he rips the Christ out of his heart and hangs him up on a cross of shame before the community—twice crucified, he has certainly committed a crime against heaven worthy of the most severe punishment.[15]

Having looked at how the emotions may be used to move an audience to action, the question must be faced as to what extent the emotion may appropriately be employed. Just how far should he go? You may think of emotional appeal in four degrees.

First, there is a *consideration of the motives* or simply talking about them. In this level of emotional appeal the speaker mentions the drives as reasons why one should act. "This action is in harmony with what you believe" (convictions); or "acting in the way that will give you a happier home" (affection and social approval).

A second degree of emotional appeal lies in *visualization of satisfaction*. Here the preacher not only suggests that a given action will satisfy a drive or remove a hindrance to one, but he paints a verbal picture of the satisfaction received from the action he is urging. "Just imagine," he says, "what joy you will feel when someone you have taught comes to Christ" (convictions, respect, and worship). Or, "Look ahead with me to the judgment. As you stand waiting, the Lord says to you, 'Well done, good and faithful servant. Thou has been faithful over a few things, I will make you faithful over many. Enter thou into

[15]Reuel Lemmons, "The Exceeding Sinfulness of Sin," *Great Sermons of 1967* (Austin: R. B. Sweet Publishing Co., 1967), 97.

the joys of thy Lord.' What a wonderful moment! And it all began with your answer to Jesus' call today" (respect and worship, self-preservation). Thus, the preacher helps his hearers to visualize the actual satisfaction which will come if the action he is urging is done.

Sometimes you will wish to go a step beyond visualizing the satisfaction to actually *stimulating the emotions*. Christianity is an emotional religion, not a philosophy of Stoicism. Christians are *supposed to feel something* when they worship, think of the Lord's death, or contemplate heaven and hell. So you certainly may want to stir the emotions of your hearers on some occasions. Sometimes you will want them to cry or laugh or to feel a strong sense of guilt, shame, or love. When properly used and controlled, such feelings are of great value in motivating the audience to a desirable action.

The fourth degree of emotional appeal might be called *inflammation of emotions*, and this level is not proper for public speeches. At this level a person has been so aroused that he cannot exert a conscious control over what he does. The use of motivation to short-circuit the more logical processes should neither be attempted nor tolerated for there is no excuse for the preacher to get listeners to do, while in a frenzy, what they would never do in the "cool light of day." Emotional appeal should never be carried to the place where it is a controlling force without restraint or where it leads to actions based on emotion alone without reason.

Yet, there definitely is a place in preaching for emotional appeal, and it is often this quality which separates the mediocre preacher from the highly successful one. A drama teacher once remarked that he judged the effectiveness of a play by whether he felt a chill down his spine, and often the preacher will find his most effective sermons are those which stir some emotion to a suitable degree.

The preacher should study very carefully the subject of motivation. He should read books on persuasion and psychology. One of his most important roles is to inspire, to motivate, to persuade; and learning to do this effectively is the work of a lifetime.

Summary

While these four functions of supporting material—interest, clarify, prove, and motivate—have been presented separately, often the same piece of supporting material may produce two or three of these effects. An example may be used primarily to prove, but may at the same time provide interest and motivation. A narration, likewise, may be used principally to motivate, but may, at the same time, clarify a statement. The important point to remember in this connection is that the speaker should have a principal objective for each bit of material which he includes, but he must also be aware of any additional values which the material may provide.

FINDING THE SUPPORTING MATERIAL

Before closing this discussion on supporting material, some attention should be given to the sources from which this material may be found and how the material should be obtained.

Sources

Every preacher who is to serve as a minister of at least average ability and effectiveness must be competent in research. This is one reason why college training of some type is important, for it is there that one best learns how and where to find materials that he needs. Some even have defined college training as the process, not of learning everything, but of learning where to find everything. Such extracurricular activities as debate and journalism are good training, too, for in these activities one must "dig" for materials and become adept at taking notes.

In his own library the preacher must have certain basic tools. He should have several translations of the Bible, a complete concordance such as Young's or Strong's, and both a current Bible dictionary and a Bible encyclopedia. If he has had enough study of the languages to use them, he should also have a Greek and a Hebrew lexicon, and of course, a standard English dictionary. A variety of commentaries is helpful and the preacher should have both sets which cover the entire Bible and those which specialize in one book or a small group of books.

Commentaries should be chosen not only on their interpretation of the Scriptures, but also on the basis of how much background of historical and cultural information they supply and how well they provide material on the organization of books and chapters. The library should also include a good general encyclopedia from which the preacher may draw historical, biographical, and artistic illustrations and data. In addition, the basic book collection for the preacher should include some works on church history, systematic theology, doctrinal issues, etiquette, and a few books for inspiration. Also of use will be some anthologies of both prose and poetry and a collection of usable quotations.

Finally, the preacher's library should include some well chosen books of sermons and perhaps sermon outlines. Special care, of course, must be taken in using these sermon materials. No preacher who relies on the sermons others have prepared will ever develop into a first-rate preacher himself. While such books of sermons will be useful for supplying ideas, illustrations, and approaches, no sermon should ever be delivered which is nothing more than a "regurgitation" of another's work. A good rule to follow in this regard is this: never preach a sermon which is based solely upon a single outline of another. If such materials are used, the preacher should always draw from more than one source and force himself to make a new outline from these materials. If he cannot present any ideas on the subject from his own independent study, at least the arrangement and development can have the stamp of his own originality. Broadus, who makes some valuable observations on this point, suggests that a preacher should "never appropriate an entire discourse, whether with or without acknowledgment."[16]

In this connection, some mention may be made of how and when to cite the sources which have been used. The source of information should be given when a speaker uses: (1) a direct quotation, (2) an important idea not part of common knowl-

---

[16]John A. Broadus. *On the Preparation and Delivery of Sermons*, rev. J. B. Weatherspoon (New York: Harper & Row Publishers, 1944), 88.

edge, (3) a striking statement for which it would be dishonest to take credit, and (4) an approach or a portion of an outline from another. This acknowledgment of a source does not weaken your influence, rather it strengthens your ethical appeal for it shows you know what others have said on the subject at hand.

The acknowledgment of sources should be made in as interesting a way as possible. When some particular source has given the germ idea for the sermon, the preacher can say, "Several weeks ago I read a statement in a book called *The Greatest Thing in the World* by Henry Drummond which has been on my mind ever since, and this idea has become the theme of the sermon today." Thus credit is given without the more formal and less interesting "footnote" type of statement.

If a quotation or paraphrase is taken from a specific author, the source should generally introduce and not follow the material. The speaker may say, for example, "Jonathan Edwards spoke on this very point in his sermon called 'Sinners in the Hands of an Angry God.'"

In writing it is important that each source be carefully documented, and the same is true in speaking; but all the documentation need not be given in the speech itself. It is useless, for example, to give minute details such as page or volume number since an audience cannot remember them. The date should be given only if it is of some particular importance.

If the author being quoted is not well known, the force of the quotation will be greater if he is identified by giving his qualifications for being an authority on the matter.

In addition to the sources of material mentioned above, the preacher should have some items which he reads regularly and which will add to his general store of knowledge and understanding as well as providing specific information, on occasion, for sermons: a daily newspaper, a weekly news magazine, and two or three religious periodicals of differing types. He should also read widely in all areas and should have some book "going" constantly. He should especially be alert for those stories that can illustrate points in a sermon and capture them in detail in permanent form.

It would be decidedly unfortunate, however, to leave the

impression that the only source for sermon ideas is the printed page. There are two other general sources which must be mentioned. The preacher should make good use of conversation with others. Frequently he will have ideas which need to be tested in the fire of conversation with other preachers and Bible scholars. On other occasions he will become the testing ground for another's ideas and from them he can learn. Whenever possible, he should associate with those whose conversation will be stimulating and informative. It is said, for example, that President Franklin Roosevelt, instead of reading a book, called the author to the White House for a conversation.

Another general source which is most important is the preacher's own experience. If some ministers spent as much time recalling situations in their own experience as they spend looking through some illustration book, they would probably find far more illustrations and more effective ones for them, for they can speak about them with more force and conviction. Of course, care should be taken not to overuse personal experiences in the pulpit; but if the preacher fears that he may be referring to himself too often, he can use occasions of which he has known personally without referring to them as such. Both good taste and Christian concern would demand, of course, that he not reveal matters which have been given to him in confidence or situations involving members of his congregation in an unpleasant or offensive way.

Making Notes

Notetaking is a most important habit for a preacher to form early in his career. He should determine some system which he wishes to use and follow it throughout his preaching life. Some like to use small notebooks which they carry with them constantly. Others prefer to carry a small pack of 3"x5" cards which can be conveniently filed.

Whatever the method, the preacher will find great value in making accurate notes. He should record all sermon ideas wherever they occur to him, in his study, on a visit, watching television, or on the golf course. Undoubtedly, every minister has conceived what he believed to be an excellent sermon plan only to have it slip his mind before it was of any use. Illustrations may occur at odd moments. One may see a dead tree being removed by the city street department and realize that this will help him emphasize a point about bearing fruit. He may see a television show on the life of Lincoln and recognize illustrative material on dedication to a cause. He may hear some speaker use an anecdote which will be useful, and, of course, he will read material in books and magazines which he will need to record. These should be preserved in detail and filed in a way that allows easy retrieval.

It is most important, however, for the preacher to remember that the item which he wishes to record is not all that must go on his note paper. The source of the information is also vital and must be placed on the same paper as the item itself. In case the information does not come from a published source, the date secured and the details of the conversation or speech heard should be recorded.

Since at least 90 per cent of what a preacher says in a sermon will be supporting material, his sermons may well stand or fall on how well he finds and uses supporting material.

ASSIGNMENT

Using Sound, Interesting, Powerful Material

Bring to class in written form to be turned in six examples of supporting materials, one from each of the six categories given. All should be taken from sermons by others. Not only should the type of the example be identified, but also its purpose (clarify, interest, prove, motivate) should be noted. The form for this assignment should be:

Statement: (the assertion in the sermon which the material is used to support)

Supporting material: (the quotation, example, facts, etc., used by the speaker)

Type: (identification of this instance as one of the six types)

Purpose: (identification as to which of the four purposes of supporting material for which the speaker was using this material)

DEVELOPING AN EXPOSITORY SERMON

(The following plan for developing an expository sermon pulls together much of the material in Chapters 3, 4, 5, 6, and 7, and demonstrates how these matters may be brought together into the process of preparing an expository sermon.)

As a wrap-up of the two chapters on organizing sermons and gathering supporting materials, let us track the step-by-step development of the common and useful expository sermon. With some adjustments, this procedure could be applied to any type of sermon. This listing will pull together many suggestions made in previous chapters and demonstrate their relationship to each other. The statements here will be in brief since these ideas are discussed more fully in other places.

I. Find the passage for the expository sermon.
   A. Ask where God's message meets man's needs.
   B. Ask whether the prospective passage deals with an issue that is both significant and practical.
   C. Draft a preliminary purpose statement to indicate the type of sermon being considered at this point, the basic content the sermon may have, and the possible outcome in terms of audience response.

II. Explore the passage.
   A. Read several translations of the passage.
   B. Study the passage from the original language to the extent that you have the skills to do so. Include in this step a consideration of the accuracy of the text.
   C. Study the context of the passage to insure that you recognize how it fits into the section and the book of which it is a part.
   D. Outline the passage to note carefully its central theme and the point it expresses about the theme.
   E. Consider related passages from elsewhere to be sure that you are interpreting this passage in har-

mony with what the Bible teaches elsewhere on the
same topic.

III. State the unique theme of the passage in a way that
relates the meaning of the passage to the need of the
audience.

A. Word the theme in the form of a subject sentence—
making the statement short, strong, and memorable.

B. Check again to be sure that you are dealing with a
lesson that is potentially biblical, interesting, practical, and significant.

C. Refine the purpose statement at this point.

IV. Word the main points.

A. Expand the theme stated as the subject sentence
into its constituent parts.

B. These parts should all bear the same relationship to
the subject sentence—that is, they should all flow
from it as lessons, challenges, steps, elements,
parties involved, reasons why, or some other consistent set of headings.

C. Use complete sentences in stating these headings.

D. State these points in parallel wording and make
them brief and striking.

E. Check each statement to see that it is true to the
meaning of the text.

F. Be sure each statement allows for further development through supporting materials.

V. Develop the main points with supporting materials.

A. Use supporting materials of a wide variety such as
quotations, comparisons, accepted truths, and fac-
tional information.

B. Use examples, whenever possible—both from the
Bible and from life—utilizing comparative, negative, and positive examples with an emphasis on
positive ones.

C. Use explanation as sparingly as possible.

D. Check to see that your points and their support are
biblical, interesting, practical, and significant.

VI. Add the introduction and conclusion.
 A. The introduction should gain attention to the subject, gain good will for the speaker, and give necessary background information for the subject.
 B. Be sure the introduction emphasizes the need you are meeting and has material that will capture interest.
 C. The conclusion should summarize and give the final motivation and appeal.
 D. The conclusion is a good place for a strong final positive example and for bringing the practical implications to a head—here is what you should do ("So what?").
VII. Consider the climax and transitions.
 A. The sermon should have rising action, peaks, and falling action. Normally there will be a sub-climax near the end of each of the main points and a major climax in the early part of the conclusion.
 B. Be sure transitions make clear the movement from point to point and keep the audience aware of the point you are developing at all times.
VIII. Check the emotional appeal in the sermon.
 A. While you should have been including materials with emotional appeals as you have developed almost all the previous steps, it is useful to review at this point to see that the sermon has sufficient emotional appeals.
 B. Ask whether your appeals are honest, fair, to the appropriate drives, and at the right level.
 IX. Make a final check for the interest level all the way through the sermon.
 A. Does your supporting material have good variety?
 B. Are there sufficient good examples?
 C. Are there practical applications and are they relevant to the lives of those in the audience?
 D. Have you drawn the audience into the sermon so they feel a part of the experience?

8 | Wording The Sermon

"Speak forth words of truth and soberness" — Acts 26:25

INTRODUCTION

Some people "have a way with words." Some speak in short, clear sentences; others in longer, complex sentences sprinkled with highly descriptive and figurative language. The word that ancient rhetoricians used to describe a speaker's characteristic use of words is *style*.

Everyone has a style—his own way of using words. Shakespeare had an elegant style filled with every type of figure of speech. Most preachers have a plain, direct style. Since the words one chooses to clothe his thoughts play such an important part in communicating ideas to the mind of the listener, the preacher must not leave his style to chance or habit. Rather, he must train himself to use words in the most effective way.

While there will and should be great variations in the style of various speakers, *there are certain qualities of style all should seek.*

CLARITY

The most basic quality of style for the preacher is clarity, for, above all else, the audience must understand his message. Since words are only symbols of the thoughts to be delivered, clarity of style actually means *transparency* so the audience may look through the words to the meaning. If the meaning may be regarded as a picture or mental image, the words must paint the picture with such clarity that the audience sees it in detail.

To achieve this clarity, the preacher must choose words which express the *exact* meaning. "Philip ran," for example, makes the picture clearer than "Philip went." "Threw," "dropped," or "stacked" is better than "placed," and "pounded" or "tapped" better than "knocked." Verbs which describe the action or movement with precision make the picture clear.

Another element of clarity is *concreteness*. While details of the "concrete-abstract continuum" must be left for writers in semantics, it is important to note here that the "fine tuner" which makes the picture sharp is the use of concrete words. All words, since they are but symbols, necessarily omit some details. That is, no word or combination of words can give *all* the details of the picture, just as no artist can include every detail in his landscape. The words that come closest to including all the details are called *concrete*, while the words which leave out the most are termed *abstract*. Notice, for example, how the picture gradually clears as this sequence of words moves from abstract to concrete: something—object—animal—mammal—canine—dog—collie—Lassie. Of course, there are uses for abstract words, but in most cases the concrete, specific word will make the picture in the mind of the auditor far more distinct.

Another aspect of clarity is the use of *specific detail*. It is often a very simple matter to include specific details in a description or narration, thus sharpening the mental image. When telling of the contest between Elijah and the Baal prophets on Mt. Carmel, for example, such details as the height of the mountain, its proximity to the sea, and its vegetation may easily assist the audience in drawing its picture: "Among all the host on the mountain top, only Elijah was an avowed servant of God;

the prophets of Baal numbered 450. He had come alone up the tree-covered hillside to stand nearly a thousand feet above the Mediterranean Sea below." Adjectives such as "rocky," "steep," "windy," "rugged," "blustering," and "colorful" should be employed to supply many needed details. Variety in the use of these words is essential: "very," "great," "beautiful," and "wonderful" are badly overused.

A final ingredient of clear style is being *concise*. Preachers often take the "long-way around" with a barrage of unnecessary words. "Now we see that in order that one may live as a Christian should, it is necessary that he be a person of faith." All of this might be said in five words: "Christians, then, must have faith." Excess verbiage fogs the understanding of the listener and is often a cover for the lack of careful thinking by the speaker. Most preachers would profit from the admonition given to the farmer whose barn was so full of hay that he had no room to milk his cows: *"Bale it."*

Clarity of style, then, may be achieved by employing exact, concrete words, by supplying specific details, and by developing conciseness. Thus, the thoughts are not only clearly perceived, but appear clothed with *energy*.

CORRECTNESS

A second quality of style to which the preacher must give attention is correctness. Many doors will be closed to the minister whose grammar is embarrassing to the congregation. Errors in agreement of subject and verb or the use of adjectives where adverbs are required will call attention to *words* rather than to *meaning*, thus erecting barriers to understanding. An audience cannot help losing respect for a man who gives his life to public speaking without taking the matter seriously enough to learn the correct use of his native tongue. While it is true that some laxity is often permitted in oral discourse which is not allowable in writing, there is no excuse for a preacher to use "I" when the objective case is required or to confuse "rise" with "raise."

VIVIDNESS

Part of Van Gogh's greatness as an artist lies in the particularly bright colors which he achieved. His paintings are memorable because they are vivid. A *vivid style* not only makes a point *clear* but makes it *interesting,* as well. A preacher can use two special elements of style to make his language colorful and vivid: *imagery* and *figures.*

Imagery simply means *making the listeners use their imaginations.* The stimulation of each of the five senses can be imaginary as well as actual so that one can "see" and "hear" a battle, smell pungent incense, feel the pain of a crown of thorns, and taste vinegar without *actually* experiencing any of these things. Imagery is best used, of course, when it *recalls experiences which have provided strong sense stimulation.* Unknown experiences must be *associated with the familiar.*

Phillips Brooks sometimes almost reached the level of poetry with his vivid imagery:

> There is a new tranquility which is not stagnation, but assurance, when a life thus enters into Christ. It is like the rushing of a million babbling, chattering mountain streams as they approach the sea and fill themselves with its deep purposes. It is like the steadying of a lost bird's quivering wings when it at last sees the nest and quiets itself with the certainty of reaching it, and settles smoothly down on level pinions to sweep unswervingly towards it. It is like these to see the calm of a restless soul that discovers Christ and rests its tired wings upon the atmosphere of His truth, and so abides in Him as it goes on towards Him.[1]

The second means for attaining vivid style is the use of *figures of speech.* Since some lists of figures run to more than two hundred, it is impossible here to discuss the subject fully; but a preacher should, by all means, take the time to study carefully in this area. The Bible itself is filled with numerous

---

[1]Quoted in Marie Hochmuth and Norman W. Mattis, "Phillips Brooks," *A History and Criticism of American Public Address* (New York: McGraw-Hill Book Co., 1943), I, 319.

figures; and, unless he is familiar with them, he will find great difficulty in properly interpreting many passages of Scripture. In learning them for purposes of exegesis, the minister will, at the same time, be learning them for use in his own preaching.

Some of the more common figures of speech include:

1. *Metaphor*—a direct comparison of things essentially un-like, a condensed comparison: "I am the door"; "Ye are the light of the world"; "This is my blood"; "You are soldiers of Christ."

2. *Simile*—a comparison of things essentially unlike using the signs of a comparison, "like" or "as": "The Christian life is like running a race"; "You are like barren fig trees, like water-less cisterns"; "We need God like sheep need a shepherd, like those in darkness need the light."

3. *Hyperbole*—an exaggeration, intended, not to deceive, but to emphasize: "Your seed will be like the stars of the heaven, the sand of the seashore"; "All Judea went out to hear John."

4. *Metonymy*—One word is put for another, such as the part for the whole, an author for his works, an adjective for the noun it commonly modifies, the cause for the effect, or the container for the contents: "As often as ye drink this *cup*"; "They have *Moses* and the *prophets*"; "Above the bright *blue*."

5. *Personification*—giving life to an inanimate object: "The stones cry out"; "The heavens declare the glory of God"; "Even the trees seemed to whisper that he was lost."

Imagery and figures of speech will give color and life to the style, but they must not be used so often that the audience begins to play a game called "find the figure" and forgets to listen to the sermon. Contrary to the opinion of some, figures of speech are not unnatural; they are natural to the person who is in the midst of strong feelings and excitement. A preacher should, therefore, use figures only when he has built up to the level of excitement when they appear natural.

A word of caution must be spoken about the use of clichés. Some figures of speech and other phrases have become so common that they are offensive to the careful listener. Who does not feel inner pain at such phrases as "caught like a rat in a trap," "as ugly as a mud fence," and "as happy as a lark"? Originality is important in the use of figures.

FORCEFULNESS

A preacher should strive for a striking, impressive, forceful style. This does not, by any means, indicate that he should seek to "impress" the audience with his ability. Rather, he should seek to *use words which will "sink in," penetrate,* and *make a memorable impression.* Some speakers have done this so well that the phrases which they coined have become a part of the language: "the iron curtain" (Churchill), "nothing to fear but fear itself" (Roosevelt), "of the people, by the people, and for the people" (Lincoln), "never have so many owed so much to so few" (Churchill).

One technique for developing memorable phrases is the use of the *balanced phrase*—a statement containing two parts which equal each other: "The gospel is the pearl of great price given by the prince of great peace"; "Abhor that which is evil; cleave to that which is good"; "Christianity exalts the individual; communism exalts the state."

Repetition is another method for impressive style. Again it is Churchill who provides the most famous example: "*We shall fight* them on the beaches; *we shall fight* them on the landing strips; *we shall fight* them in the cities." One might summarize an expository sermon from Ephesians by saying: "Walking worthily, then, means walking in love, walking in peace, walking in good works, walking in Jesus' steps, and walking as children of light." Repeating a word or phrase in successive clauses plants the idea deeply.

Alliteration can also make a statement impressive, but care must be taken not to overuse this method. Some preachers make every main heading in every sermon begin with the same letter. While this is effective when used carefully, its effect is lost when it is overdone. One may, for example, speak of the church in prophecy, in performance, and in perfection, and of the twin sins of arrogance and avarice. One also may speak of the "pitiful prospects for peace" and the "double-dealing of the devil." A sermon on seven P's from the devil's "P Patch" with a list of seven sins all starting with "P" is probably providing a potential problem.

ORIGINALITY

Though a preacher will wish, on some occasions, to quote useful statements from others, he should work to develop his own style. He should assiduously avoid the threadbare clichés common among preachers and speakers: "Last but not least"; "And in conclusion I would like to say"; "Thank you for your kind attention"; "Now I said all that to say this"; "We find that"; "Let us look to John the fourth chapter and about the fifth verse"; "While we stand and sing."

CONCLUSION

One final word should be said about style. There is a great difference between written and oral style. Often a preacher will write out a sermon and then speak aloud what sounded good on paper only to deliver a sermon that is distant and "over the heads" of the audience.

The oral style is less formal. It has shorter sentences and uses more familiar words. It has a spontaneity about it that is different than carefully crafted written language.

Looked at from the opposite point of view, a transcribed speech that sounded great often reads poorly because there will be incomplete sentences, repetition, and informal words.

It is for this reason that a sermon written in advance usually does not sound right to an audience. Of course, it is good to carefully draft key sentences and phrases. It is also helpful sometimes to write out short sections of a sermon to polish the language. In delivering the sermon, however, the preacher should be sure to keep good eye contact with the audience and to retain the sense of spontaneity.

Audiences do not like to be aware of long preparation for a speech. As long ago as the fourth century before Christ, Demosthenes, a great Greek orator, was accused of having speeches that "smelled of the lamp" because they were so highly polished.

A preacher will best develop his own style by first under-standing the various qualities and techniques of style as pre-sented here and elaborated elsewhere. Then he should read and listen with particular attention to word choice and word combinations. Writing, with its opportunity for reworking and polishing, affords an excellent opportunity for training toward good and original style. Correctness and clarity should come first; vividness and force should follow. After years of practice comes originality.

ASSIGNMENT

Wording the Sermon

Prepare a ten-minute sermon for delivery in class. Prepare a full outline to hand in prior to delivery. Be sure to prepare the sermon to represent one of the organizational types in Chapter 6. In addition, a complete technical plot should be prepared as you develop your outline which reveals your strategy for all parts of the sermon. See the outline at the end of Chapter 3 for a sample technical plot.

This sermon should also show carefully polished language. Use some figures of speech and some well-turned phrases. You may even wish to write a few opening and closing sentences in full. Be sure, however, that your delivery shows good eye contact with the audience and has a "sense of directness" in delivery.

9 | **Delivering Powerfully**

"Speak boldly, as I ought to speak"
— Ephesians 6:20

INTRODUCTION

Opinions vary widely on the subject of sermon delivery. Some would say, "As long as a man has the truth, it does not matter how he says it." These would point to 1 Corinthians 2:1 where Paul states that he "came not with excellency of speech" and to 2 Corinthians 11:6 where he claimed to be "rude in speech." They would argue that if Paul did not need to use "high-flown" delivery, neither should one today.

Others would argue in reply that Apollos is described favorably as an "eloquent man" (Acts 18:24) and that an analysis of Paul's sermons shows clearly that he did employ both rhetorical and psychological principles. His reference to a lack of excellency in speech, they claim, was not intended to indicate that he gave no regard to clear, vigorous, effective delivery, but that in contrast to the Greek sophists, who were common in his day, he made no attempt at their flowery, overdone manner of eloquence.

It is true, of course, that the systematic application of the principles of rhetoric to Christian preaching came several hundred years after the apostolic age. Paul, however, makes it clear that he is completely in favor of a delivery which allows a clear presentation which is easily grasped by the audience. In 1 Corinthians 14, he emphasizes the importance of speaking so the audience can comprehend: "So also ye, unless ye utter by the tongue speech easy to be understood, how shall it be known what is spoken?" In Ephesians 6:20, moreover, Paul writes that he will "speak boldly, as I ought to speak."

To say the least, then, the New Testament allows and even encourages attention to delivery, not so that the speaker himself can be praised or so that the message of the gospel will appear to stand in the wisdom of man, but so that the Word of God may be brought forcefully upon the hearts of men.

Observation of preachers and churches will confirm the need for preachers who can clearly and vigorously speak the truths of the gospel. Poor delivery not only kills interest, it obscures truth. The preacher may join Aristotle in regarding delivery as a regrettable necessity (*Rhetoric 3.1*), or he may agree with Demosthenes who said that the first, second, and third laws of effective speaking were "delivery, delivery, delivery." But in either case, effective delivery must be regarded as essential for excellence in the pulpit. Good delivery can make the average sermon listenable and the good sermon excellent. On the other hand, poor delivery makes even the best message weak and ineffective.

UTILIZING THE VOICE

Many of the aspects of making full utilization of the voice in delivering the sermon are almost too obvious to mention and certainly do not require elaboration. The preacher must speak *loudly enough* to be heard by "the deaf man in the back row"; he must *articulate carefully* enough for his words to be understood easily; he must *pronounce his words* in an acceptable manner. There are many other considerations, however, which are sometimes overlooked: *attaining vocal variety, utilizing the voice for emphasis and climax, and avoiding an unnatural "preacher tone."*

1. *Attaining Vocal Variety.* One of the most essential requisites for interesting preaching is variety of voice. The preacher who speaks at the same speed and loudness throughout the sermon will often find he has been more of a sandman than a preacher. There are only four factors of voice which can be varied and from changes in these comes all vocal variety: *rate, volume, pitch, and quality.*

Rate in voice refers to the *speed* at which the words are spoken. The rate is controlled both by the *length of time taken to speak each word* and the *space left between words*. Both of these should take longer when a speaker wishes to emphasize while at other times he may toss a sentence off quickly to break the intensity. The *pause* between words also is of great importance. A pause is a period of silence planned for a specific purpose while a hesitation is a momentary loss of control. The pause can be used to accomplish many aims: (1) *before* an important word, to "plant" it or show it has unusual significance; (2) *after* a word, to let it "sink in"; (3) *after* a sentence or climax, to give a moment of rest before starting the next area of thought. The pause, then, achieves much of what the use of space, indentations, italics, and underlining accomplish in printing.

Rate is, perhaps, the simplest of the variable factors of voice to control, and preachers who recognize a problem in variety should start with a conscious attempt to attain variety in speed. They can practice a paragraph, learning to emphasize key ideas by slowing down, by pauses in key places, and by speaking less important parts more rapidly.

Volume must also be changed throughout the speech, for maintaining a constant level of loudness will very quickly tire the audience. Since a louder volume is often associated with emphasis, a constant loudness appears to the audience as an attempt to give everything equal emphasis. It is axiomatic that when everything is emphasized, nothing is emphasized. Increases in volume are essential to building a climax, and the preacher must save his loudness for the points of special emphasis. It should also be noted that since emphasis comes from *change,* not loudness alone, a low volume can often be used effectively for emphasis. Thus if the preacher has been moving at a rather fast rate and high volume, the sudden change to a slow, soft sentence will be especially striking.

Pitch refers to highs and lows on the musical scale. Not many persons actually speak on only one pitch or as a monotone. Such would be unbearable for any length of time. *The most common error in connection with pitch is the repetition of the same series of pitches.* Thus some preachers begin each sentence in the entire sermon about the middle of their vocal range, then give a slight, gradual glide upward, and near the end of the phrase or sentence, a sharp drop. This may be diagrammed as follows:

I wish to make it clear, that before one can be born again

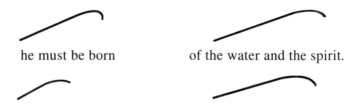

he must be born   of the water and the spirit.

Others have a pattern which is continually downward:

I wish to make it clear, that before one can be born again

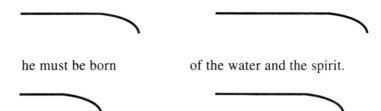

he must be born   of the water and the spirit.

The repetition of the same inflectional pattern in this fashion is one of the most frequent problems in preaching, and every preacher should check himself and have competent critics check him to see that he avoids this. Once the pattern is established it is very difficult to break. The best method of improvement is the use of an audio or video recorder and regular practice with a skilled observer.

Variations in *quality* or vocal timbre are also possible, though they are less consciously used than other variations. Perhaps this is most easily seen in the use of sarcasm as the voice is given the particular tone associated with the sarcastic. Variations in quality will usually come automatically with variations in rate, volume, and pitch and with a mental response to the meaning of what is being spoken. Sincerity, vigor, and enthusiasm in voice are largely matters of quality, too, and are of fundamental importance in gaining the desired response from the audience. A good actor learns to use these subtle variations by "thinking the thought" to establish the mood and this, in turn, gives the voice the proper quality.

2. *Utilizing the Voice for Emphasis and Climax.* Closely related to variety in voice are the matters of emphasis and climax. *Emphasis* is the placing of special force on a word, phrase, or sentence, in order to call attention to it and underscore its significance. In the sentence "God is love," for example, emphasis should fall upon the words "God" and "love," for the verb "is" does not require special attention. In the sentence "He *is* the one," however, emphasis may well be placed on the word "is" to indicate that without doubt, "He is the one." The particular word emphasized will often affect the entire meaning of the sentence. In the simple question "Are *you* going to town?" if the emphasis is placed on "you" the sentence means "Are *you* (as opposed to he) going to town?" But if force is placed on "*town*," the sentence means "Are you going to *town*?" (as opposed to the country). This emphasis is, of course, applied as rate; volume, pitch, and quality are changed to place force upon a particular word or phrase.

Climax refers, not to emphasis on a specific word, but to a trend of the voice established by the combination of these factors for variety. As rate, volume, and pitch are increased gradually, the voice moves toward a climax, and a whole *series of climaxes* should lead to *the one big moment in the entire sermon.* In other terms, the audience is led along a trail of peaks and valleys until they come, at last, to the highest peak of the range. This climax in delivery should, of course, correspond to the emotional and/or intellectual climax in the sermon.

The preacher should plan for the points of intermediate and final climax in a sermon. These should not be left to chance for they may, then, not develop at all.

Just as a musician will plan a piece of music to have a point of highest crescendo and a dramatist will have a peak for the rising action, so the preacher should develop his plan for the series of climaxes that culminate in the point of greatest impact.

3. *Avoiding the Unnatural "Preacher Tone."* Many preachers have fallen into a use of the voice which is sometimes called a "preacher tone" or "sanctimonious wail." While some young preachers have purposely attempted to develop such a delivery in order to sound like their "idol," the practice should be avoided since it is distracting to the audience and keeps the preacher from using emphasis and climax as they should be used. While it is easy to determine whether a preacher has this problem, the cause and cure are not so easily discovered. Usually there is a *repeated pattern of inflection*, as shown above, with a *constancy of rate*. Sometimes the preacher has also affected a *voice quality* which he "uses" only when he preaches, and some have even developed, in addition to their natural voice, a special "voice" for preaching and another for praying. There is no reason for a preacher to sound unlike himself or other human beings when he preaches and a special, unnatural use of the voice will hinder, not help, his development.

4. *Care of the Voice.* Since the preacher's work centers largely in the use of his voice, he should make a diligent effort to learn to use it well. Above this, moreover, he should make every effort to protect it. He should not speak when he is suffering with laryngitis or extreme vocal fatigue, and he should be alert to any chronic voice problems. Since most problems of voice arise either from respiratory infection or allergic conditions, the preacher should be especially careful with such problems. The voice is a delicate instrument and can be damaged permanently by misuse.

UTILIZING THE BODY

The audience not only *hears*, it also *sees* the speaker. For some, this is unfortunate; for others, it provides the opportunity to make the presentation more effective. The principal thing to be stressed is that the body should be alert and responsive, just as the audience is supposed to be. A listener can pay surface attention with no response; so can a speaker. The extreme example would be a preacher who reads a manuscript in a way which indicates that he is not actually conscious of what he is reading. *Since an audience will tend to respond to what is spoken in the same way the speaker does, the preacher should appear alert, active, and energetic.*

The preacher's *body language* should add to the spoken message, not detract from it. When he is urging action, he should move enthusiastically; when he is calling for prayer, his body and voice will be subdued. His *face*, likewise, should reflect the emotional overtones of the message. Some movement about the platform provides relief, and gestures may be used to emphasize and clarify.

As any actor knows, the position and movement of the body have a language all their own. One can, by leaning toward the audience and turning his palms upward, express an invitation. By leaning backwards and holding his palms outward, he expresses repulsion. A hand in the pocket and a casual posture expresses informality while an erect, upright posture behind the pulpit stand suggests formality.

The use of the microphone affects delivery considerably. Before the use of public address systems, speakers had to generate enough volume to be heard by large numbers and even their softer points were still very loud. With the microphone came the opportunity for "conversational delivery," because even soft volume could still be heard. But microphones anchored the speaker to one spot, curtailing movement about the platform.

Now with lavalieres and cordless microphones, the opportunity to move about the platform has been returned to the arsenal of the preacher and he will likely wish to take advantage of it. Making the position behind a stand his basic location, the preacher may move to the side of and even in front of the stand. Each movement, however, should be motivated. The movement from behind the stand and forward toward the audience can help to build toward a climax and give the preacher a warmer relationship with the audience.

The point here is not, of course, to present the possible meaning for every movement, body stance, or hand position. Rather, the point is that each of these has a meaning which the audience, unconsciously, reads and the speaker should, therefore, use them cautiously.

The preacher also should *avoid distractions* coming from his gestures or movement or facial expression. Pacing back and forth, using the same gesture over and over, folding the hands as if in prayer, rapping on the pulpit—all these and similar distractions should be avoided. The body, the voice, and the words should all work together in the communication of both idea and mood.

It goes without saying, of course, that a preacher should be *dressed neatly* and *rather conservatively.* Dress in this fashion is important, not necessarily for what it adds, but for the distraction generally resulting from slovenly or extreme dress.

EXTEMPORANEOUS OR MANUSCRIPT DELIVERY

There are essentially only two types of delivery from the point of view of *when* the exact wording of the speech is done: *before* the speech and *during* the speech. When the exact wording, except for such items as main headings or an opening and closing sentence, is left for the moment of utterance, the delivery is termed *extemporaneous.* This word means "out of the time" or "at the time." Contrary to a popular notion, an extemporaneous speech is not necessarily one which is spoken without preparation. It may be carefully prepared with supporting material gathered and a complete outline made. The extemporaneous speech, however, is not written out ahead of time; rather, *the exact choice of words is left for the time of delivery.* The amount of preparation, then, is not a determining quality of an extemporaneous speech. It is, rather, one in which most of the exact wording is done *as the speech is given.*

The other type is usually called a *manuscript sermon*, that is, the *wording is written down before the speech is delivered.* On some occasions the manuscript is read and on others the words are *memorized.* Some combination of these may also be used.

While both types have advantages and disadvantages, for the most part, the preacher will find much better results from extemporaneous speaking. When he researches and outlines his speech before the time and then words it as it is delivered, he is able to look at the audience and establish a strong rapport through eye contact. He also will sound more natural and will have that spontaneous vigor which an audience finds appealing.

The manuscript sermon, on the other hand, has the advantage of attaining a higher excellence of style, since the words can be chosen before they are written into final form. The use of figures of speech and polished phrasing can also be accomplished more easily in this type of speech. The manuscript speech, however, is beset with pitfalls. There is a natural prejudice against listening to a speech which is read from a manuscript and, for a preacher, to memorize each sermon is too time-consuming to be feasible. The delivery of a memorized speech is also likely to leave much to be desired in terms of natural, enthusiastic delivery. Adaptation to immediate circumstances, moreover, is all but impossible when the speech has been worded completely in advance.

There are some who write out portions of a sermon while speaking other parts extemporaneously. If you can write in "oral style" and can speak the manuscript portion without sounding "canned" and while making only casual glances at the text, you might find this plan effective.

All in all, however, extemporaneous delivery will serve most preachers as the most effective style. It is good to work out the exact statement of the main headings, perhaps the opening and closing sentence, and some of the figures of speech to be used. These, like quotations and other supporting material, will be woven into the speech as it is delivered. It should be added that practice in delivering the speech will help to establish some of the phrasing and will make the words come more easily— especially for the inexperienced preacher. "Preaching to the stumps" is highly recommended before the actual delivery of the sermon. Even some of the most experienced preachers may occasionally be found in their pulpit, preaching to empty pews as a means of preparation for Sunday services.

Good delivery is essential. A congregation wants to be proud of its preacher's speaking and will more readily bring others when this is so. The message will get "through" to the listener when the delivery strengthens rather than diminishes the impact of the words spoken. To improve his delivery, a speaker should use audio and video tape for self-analysis and occasionally ask a trusted and experienced preacher to give him advice.

ASSIGNMENT

Delivering Powerfully

Prepare for class delivery a sermon with a full technical plot on the outline. Give particular attention to the matters of wording, voice, and body that have been studied in the last two chapters.

10 | Preaching For Special Occasions

Three preaching situations need some special consideration: weddings, funerals, and baccalaureate sermons. While the methods discussed previously apply to these events, they are somewhat different and will take special preparation.

WEDDINGS

A wedding is a ceremonial occasion and, while the cry against "big weddings" is sometimes heard, there is something good to be said for making the occasion of marriage as important as possible. Since marriage as an institution is losing importance to many, those who believe that marriage should be permanent should make the wedding occasion one of solemnity, beauty, and significance.

The preacher will find the following list helpful as he thinks about the responsibility of performing a wedding ceremony.

1. *Marriage Counseling.* When a minister is asked to per-

form a wedding ceremony, he should inform the couple that marriage counseling is part of his regular procedure. Unless they have already had substantial marriage counseling, he should insist that he have two to four sessions with them. A minister should have, of course, some training in counseling as a part of his preparation. For those who are not certain of what to do in such counseling, the following list may be of some benefit in planning the meetings.

a. Be sure that the couple has the right to marry both legally and scripturally.

b. Discuss the responsibilities of the husband and of the wife to each other and the meaning of love for each other as "constant unselfishness."

c. Discuss the following areas to avert possible conflicts and problems later on: (1) relationship to each couple's parents, (2) financial plans, (3) housing plans, (4) communication, (5) handling finances, (6) doing things together, and (7) making decisions together.

d. Discuss the place of expressing affection and of love-making in the marriage and be certain that the couple has adequate information on sexual relations and birth control. You do not have to provide this personally but should provide suitable material and/or see that they get it from others.

e. Discuss the spiritual aspects of a good home and help the couple lay their plans for a spiritually active home.

f. If necessary, spend time studying the Bible with the couple to bring them into a good relationship with Christ before the marriage.

g. Discuss the wedding plans and be sure that the bride has the plans well made before the rehearsal. Otherwise, the rehearsal may be a time of frustration and even controversy. The bride should be in charge at the rehearsal, and you should be present only to walk through your part and explain what the wedding party will do during your wedding sermon. Include in this discussion the legal requirements such as when and where to get the marriage license.

2. *Be Sure You Are Licensed.* The requirement for being licensed to perform weddings varies from state to state, but the preacher must be certain that he is legally authorized before acting in this capacity. He should check with the County Clerk for details. Before performing a ceremony he should have the marriage license in hand and check it carefully to determine that all is in order. He will create a very embarrassing situation if he performs a ceremony after the license is no longer valid or in a place where the license is not good.

3. *Prepare the Wedding Sermon.* The wedding sermon should be brief, simple, impressive, solemn, and somewhat elevated in style. The preacher should call to mind, both for the bride and groom and for the audience, the meaning and divine plan for marriage; but the wedding is not the place for arguing about controversial details. The occasion should be planned to give dignity and satisfaction to the beginning of a new home and should, therefore, leave everyone feeling optimistic and happy about the occasion. The ceremony will typically have seven parts: introduction, giving of the bride by the father, comments on marriage, the vows, the rings, the pronouncement, and the prayer. Songs will sometimes be interspersed.

The following ceremony is given in full to demonstrate some of the details about weddings: an appropriate length, a possible form for the vows, the point at which the father typically gives the bride away, and something of the style to be achieved.

Sample Marriage Ceremony

I. Introduction:
    We have gathered today to witness the union of these two in the bonds of marriage. Marriage has been instituted by God, approved by Christ, and regulated by the Holy Spirit, and is intended for the benefit of mankind. It is good, therefore, that these two, finding in each other those qualities which they believe desirable, should wish to enter this union.

II. Who giveth this woman to be married? (Father: "I do" or "Her mother and I.")

III. Comments on Marriage:

Marriage is a great adventure, a time for joy and sorrow, victory and defeat, hope and despair. But through all of these, you will find strength and consolation from each other. If you successfully pursue this venture, you will receive the benefits of a useful life and glorious hereafter.

The Bible tells you how to have a successful marriage. It recommends love as the guide for your journey together. Paul wrote to the Ephesians: "Husbands love your wives as Christ also loved the church and gave himself up for it" (Ephesians 5:25). And to Titus, he wrote that the young women were to be taught to love their husbands (Titus 2:4).

First of all, this love you are to have for each other has in it an element of friendship. You are to enjoy each other's company. Plan to do many things together and build many good times and special events into your relationship. This will provide a base that will hold you close when difficult winds blow.

Second, this love you share should have in it a strong element of unselfishness. Love means that each of you takes more joy in giving than receiving, more joy in serving than in being served, more joy in praising than in being praised. This element of love keeps your relationship strong and growing.

Third, the love you have for each other is to be romantic. God made us to enjoy the touch of the one we love and has said that husbands and wives are to have a relationship that is so close and so permanent that they alone may enjoy the special intimacies of husband and wife.

So your love means a close friendship, a strong unselfishness, and a warm, tender, caring relationship that will last for a lifetime.

The Bible also teaches that for us to be successful in any venture in this life, we must have love for God; and this means strong ties to Jesus and His people.

The closer you get to God, the closer He will bring

you to each other. Remember that God is a part of the covenant you are making today, a third member of this union. With this love for God and for each other as your constant guide, you will be able to pass through the rapids of life and someday reach the peaceful sea of eternity.

The Holy Spirit also teaches that a marriage built on the love we have described will be as permanent as the lives of the two who enter this union, that the marriage will be as sacred as the bonds which unite Christ and His church, and that the tie between husband and wife will be even closer than that between parent and child.

IV. Vows:

You are now to repeat vows pledging to take each other and promising to live according to God's teaching on marriage. These vows are not to be mere form, but are to be the sincere expression of your heart for each other as you enter this divine covenant.

Do you, (man), take (woman) to be your wedded wife; to love, honor, and cherish; in sickness and health; in prosperity and adversity; living with her according to God's laws of marriage until death do you part? ("I do.")

And do you, (woman), take (man) to be your wedded husband; to love, honor, cherish, and obey; in sickness and health; in prosperity and adversity; living with him according to God's laws of marriage, until death do you part? ("I do.")

V. Rings:

Rings are to be given as tokens of the covenant you make today with each other and with God. Just as in ancient times a covenant was sealed with the exchange of gifts, so today you ratify this covenant with these rings. May these rings always be symbols of your love for each other and a remembrance of this occasion.

To the groom: "With this ring I thee wed, and with my worldly goods and my heart's fondest affection, I thee endow." (Repeat for bride.)

VI. Pronouncement:
     Inasmuch as you have taken these vows, by the
     authority vested in me as a minister of the gospel by this
     state, I pronounce you husband and wife, and what God
     has joined together, let not man put asunder (Matthew
     19:6). (Kiss)
VII. Prayer.

4. *Attend the Rehearsal*. Usually the night before a wedding
there is a wedding rehearsal. The bride, typically, is in charge
at the rehearsal, and you are there to walk through your part of
the service. She should have planned in advance when each
song will be sung, when each one comes in, and where each one
will stand. A listing and a drawing of this done in advance can
be very helpful if there are several attendants.

Your part at the rehearsal will be to practice with the others
when you come in and where you will stand. Then you will talk
the wedding party through your part about the father giving
away the bride, the rings, the kiss, and when to start the
recessional.

You should know enough about standard wedding procedure
to be able to advise on such things as the bride's side of the
audience being on the right or that when doing a unity candle the
bride and groom usually blow out their individual candles
leaving only the one central candle burning. At the rehearsal
you should tell the groom and the best man that you will need
the marriage license before the ceremony and cannot begin
without it.

5. *At the Wedding*. You will want to arrive early enough to
give assurance that you will be in your place. You will need to
receive the marriage license and check it prior to the wedding.
After the ceremony, complete the license. If there is a place for
witnesses, the best man and the maid of honor are good ones to
ask to sign since they were specially chosen by the bride and the
groom. Be sure to mail the license soon to the proper authority.
Normally you should also attend the reception.

6. *After the Wedding*. If the couple is living in your city, you
should pay them a visit a couple of weeks after the wedding.

This can help their ties with the church and give them spiritual encouragement. Also, they may have a need to discuss something about their adjustment with you.

FUNERALS

A funeral is one of the most difficult situations in the work of the minister. Since both he and the audience will be under unusual emotional strain, he will have to be especially certain that he has planned well for the occasion.

As soon as the preacher learns of a death among those he knows, he should visit the family and offer whatever assistance he can. Oftentimes the family will be too upset to think clearly, and he will need to help them get their plans organized. In rendering such assistance, he must, of course, be especially understanding and should avoid pressing himself where he is not needed or wanted. Particularly a local minister should not assume that one of his families will want him to speak at a funeral. They may have asked someone else years before. The last thing a grieving family needs to have to worry about is the feelings of the local preacher. The minister will wish to check with the funeral director on details of the funeral itself if he is to be directly involved.

The funeral service is held principally to (1) pay respect to the dead, (2) comfort the survivors, and (3) warn the living; and these aims should be in the mind of the preacher as he prepares his address.

In paying respect to the dead, the preacher will need to take special note of the spiritual state of the deceased (1) as unaccountable and, therefore, a "safe" infant or child, (2) as a faithful Christian who has a strong basis for hope, or (3) as a backslider or non-Christian regarding whom the preacher does not wish to speak with hope of heaven. The spiritual condition of the person should have great bearing on what the preacher says at the funeral, for he must not belie his regular preaching by what he says at a funeral. To do so is to be a hypocrite. He can begin his thinking, then, by determining into which of the following categories he will regard the deceased for purposes of this sermon:

1. In the case of the infant or small child, the preacher should be able to give excellent comfort to the parents by reference to such passages as Matthew 19:13, 14; 18:1-4; Luke 18:15-17; and 2 Samuel 12:23. Since the New Testament everywhere indicates that responsible obedience is required to obtain heaven, only those capable of such are held accountable. While the death of a small child is often a great disappointment and sorrow, consolation can be offered by reference to the eternal destiny of the child. Indeed, if the parents were seeking to lead their children toward heaven, the death of a child is an occasion of absolute certainty that their dream has been realized.

2. When the decedent was a faithful Christian, so far as the preacher knows, he may be optimistic about the future with the use of some of these Scriptures: Psalms 1; 15; 23; 90:10; 116:15; Proverbs 31:10; John 11:25, 26; 14:1-6; Romans 8:26-39; 1 Corinthians 15:12-26, 50-58; 2 Corinthians 4:16-18; 5:1-8; 1 Thessalonians 4:13-18; 2 Timothy 4:7, 8; Revelation 14:13; 21:1-7; 22:12-14. He certainly should speak of the hope Christians have as an encouragement to those remaining. Paul, in fact, says we should "comfort" one another in time of death (1 Thessalonians 4:13-17).

3. When the preacher is called on to speak at the funeral of one about whom there is doubt or uncertainty as to his spiritual state or whose condition is obviously without hope, he must resist the natural pressure to comfort beyond what the Scriptures might authorize. His safest course is to speak of some good personal qualities the person had, state plainly that what is said at the funeral can neither add nor detract to God's measure of the person, and suggest that he is in the hands of a just and merciful God. He may wish to make the additional point that if the deceased were able to give a message to those who remain, it undoubtedly would be to make preparations for the time when each of those still living will have to pass over the river of death. In other words, when the preacher feels it is not in harmony with his regular preaching to give hope for heaven about a deceased, he should not offer such hope. He may still, however, say good things about the deceased personally and may state the truth that the deceased is in the hands of a just and

merciful God.

By paying proper respect to the dead, the preacher will, of course, be giving some comfort to the survivors, but he can do even more. Certainly if he can give reasonable hope for the deceased, he should by all means give it. He also should comfort by placing death in the Christian perspective of life and eternity. The contrast between Christian hope in the resurrection and the hopelessness of heathen religions can be comforting to believers. The conduct of others who have faced well the time of death also is of value.

The warning to the living also is an important part of every funeral service. While it must be discreet, every person present should be called upon to review his own readiness for such an event. While the service should not be focused on evangelism or repentance, it should bring all to think of their own spiritual state.

One useful technique for funeral sermons is to try to think of passages which the deceased's life calls to mind or illustrates, and to make these passages the central focus of the message. A good father, for example, might recall to our minds Ephesians 6:4; a good mother, Proverbs 31. A good businessman might bring to mind Ephesians 4:28; a worker in benevolence, Acts 9:36-42; and a personal worker, Acts 8:4. A few minutes of thought will turn up several appropriate passages for any person, whether a Christian or not, and these can become the main headings of the funeral comments. The first of the two samples below uses this approach. The samples also demonstrate how to deal honestly with the circumstances, to make respectful reference to the deceased, and to keep the remarks centered on Scripture.

Another useful technique is to find one or more Bible characters with whom to associate the deceased. Points of the sermon can be the points of comparison or even a series of characters with whom the comparison is made.

One more suggestion about funeral sermons is that most audiences at funerals like to hear the preacher retell some incidents in the life of the deceased or recall qualities that he/she had with examples. Thus, the minister should make the funeral sermon personal with references to the deceased. If he is not well enough acquainted personally to have such information, he can get it by visiting with others. Often in his visit with the family of the deceased, they will enjoy retelling some of their favorite occasions. This will both be useful for the preacher and good therapy for the family. Often the incidents will be humorous and the family will laugh when retelling them. It is not inappropriate to use such incidents in a funeral sermon. More such humor is now being used in funerals.

The preacher will normally have four basic elements to work together in his comments: (1) the obituary, usually available from the funeral director or the newspaper, (2) Scripture readings, (3) appropriate comments, and (4) prayer. Sometimes all of these will be part of a single address. At other times the preacher will wish to have the first section of his presentation for the obituary, a Scripture, a prayer followed by a song, and then, as a second section, he will make his main comments and have a prayer. Sometimes two different ministers will share in the service with one doing the first section mentioned and the other doing the second.

The Death of a Saint

Purpose: To stimulate the bereaved to joy and the living to service so that the death of this person may serve to bring others closer to God.

Introduction:

- A. Most funerals are sad occasions, but this one really is not. Of course, all of us are sad that we will not see _____ for the time being, but this sadness is overcome by our joy that she has gone home to rest from her labors. Her soul had become too great to be held in her frail body, and it has been released to join the Lord, whom she loved and served.
- B. It was for just such occasions as this that Paul told the Thessalonians not to sorrow as those who have no hope (1 Thessalonians 4:13).

Subject Sentence: As I look at her death today, I am made to think of three great truths.

Body:

I. "Whosoever would be great among you, let him be your servant" (Matthew 20:26).

    A. _____ served her community (examples).

    B. But more important than these public deeds are the many private acts of unselfish service which she performed (examples).

    C. The most important part of her useful life, however, was her contribution to the kingdom of God, which she dearly loved. Without question, if she could point to that in her life which now seems the most important, her work for God would stand as uppermost (examples).

II. "Precious in the sight of Jehovah is the death of his saints" (Psalms 116:15).

    A. We cannot, of course, speak for God; and none of us is the judge of his fellowman; but for those who have lived a faithful Christian life, we have the assurance that death for them is not a tragic ending of life, but the beautiful beginning of eternity.

    B. From our side, death seems a dark door through which one passes into an unknown room of mystery. From the glimpse which God has given us of what lies beyond, however, when death is viewed from the other side, it is the golden door which takes one from this life of sorrow, sickness, and distress, to a life of glory, beauty, and rest.

    C. When Paul came to the end of his life, he could say: 2 Timothy 4:6-8.

    D. I am sure that _____ can say, "It is better now," and as we gather today, it is not to mourn her passing, but to honor her life and to rededicate ourselves to the kind of life she lived.

III. "Watch therefore, for ye know not the day nor the hour" (Matthew 25:13).

    A. When I think of the useful life and the precious death of _____, I am led, not to weep for her, but to weep for my own weakness and failings.

B. It is on occasions like this that we are often able to see all of life in a truer perspective. Engulfed in the day's activities, we may lose sight of what is truly important, just as the sailor may be so busy stoking the fire to make his ship go faster, that he forgets to look at the compass which tells him where he is going.

C. As her life and death should show us, the most important part of life is to live for God. On occasions like this, everything fades into nothing except that which is done in service to God.

D. I want to live so that when I lie before the assembly and someone stands where I now stand, he can say of me, as I can say of her, he lived for God and used his energy and his talents to spread the kingdom.

Conclusion:

A. In these good, Christian qualities, let us be as she was.

B. Prayer

Funeral Sermon
(For one who lived an upright life,
but was not a faithful Christian)

1. We have come today to honor this relative and friend. On behalf of the family, I wish to thank you for coming.

2. Obituary.

3. Message:

Introduction: As we hear this brief summary of_____'s achievements, we can see a theme that ran through all aspects of his life—he was a man who served. The Bible tells us that service should be the key to our lives. Jesus said, "I came not to be ministered unto but to minister." Jesus also said, "Whosoever shall be greatest among you, let him be your servant."

Notice some of the ways _____ served.

I. He served his country as a soldier.

He was in the army in WWII, giving four years of his life to help protect our freedom as a nation. Those of us who lived during those years know that not only was the freedom of our nation, but the freedom of the world was at stake in that war. His service to the nation is a noble work and reason to honor and thank him today.

II. He served young people as a teacher.

He began a long teaching career in a one-room school in Oklahoma and later taught for thirty-one years at the University of _____. He retired from there in 1978. To make his work as a teacher the very best he could make it, he spent many years in preparation. He received not only a bachelor's degree from X, but a masters from X and a doctorate from X—one of the top universities in the nation.

A career as a teacher is very rewarding—if you like to serve. It does not pay the highest salaries and it is not the easiest work to do, but it is a rich work if you like to see young people grow and blossom before your eyes. As a teacher, _____ loved to see the abilities of young people develop under his instruction.

_____'s work as a teacher is noble work and for it, we honor and thank him today.

III. He served his family as a generous and cheerful relative.

Since he was older than his two sisters, he took them on trips to give them a good time and to help educate them. Although he never married, he loved children and liked to play with them at family gatherings. He liked to reward those in the family who made some notable achievement.

His service to his family is a noble work, and for it we honor and thank him today.

Conclusion: From _____, then, we can learn a great lesson in service. From him, too, we learn that all of us are here but a few years at best and we must make the most of these years in serving others. This is a noble way to spend a life.

_____, like all of us, will stand before a just and loving God to give account of his life. For that moment, all of us must make the best preparation we can by serving others and by obeying Jesus Christ, whom God sent to be our Savior. It is not our place today to predict how God will judge any of us, but it is our place to use this solemn moment to let _____'s life remind us of two great truths: We will all be judged on the basis of how we have spent our lives, and serving others should be an important part of each life.

Let us close this service now with a reading of Scripture and a prayer.

Reading of 23rd Psalm.

4. Prayer

The graveside service which follows the funeral should be brief. The minister should read a passage such as Ecclesiastes 12, John 5:25-29, Psalm 23, or 1 Thessalonians 4:13-18, and follow the reading with a prayer. After this, he should speak briefly to the near kin and possibly escort them to the car if he is especially well acquainted with the family.

Proper procedure calls for the preacher to walk ahead of the casket whenever it is taken out of the building and when carried from the funeral car to the grave. He also generally stands at the head of the casket while those present view the body, if this is to be part of the service.

After the funeral he should leave quietly and return home, but should not consider his duties done until he has called on the family the following day.

BACCALAUREATES / COMMENCEMENTS

Many schools, sometimes even public schools, have a special service for graduates which can focus on moral and spiritual issues. While the preacher should not take advantage of this situation to "push his church," he should place a strong emphasis on spiritual needs and challenges and seek to inspire. The following example shows how this might be done.

Three Great Teenagers

Purpose: To stimulate the graduating class to greater interest in spiritual things so that they will live closer to God.

Introduction:

    A. It is an honor to be included in your plans at this

important time in your life.

B. As you leave high school, some of you will go on to college, others will enter some kind of business, others work on farms, others get married, but the principles which I wish to mention tonight will fit in any situation.

Subject Sentence: I would like to tell you of three great Bible characters who as teenagers displayed the qualities I hope you will have.

Body:

I. David, as a teenager, defeated Goliath.
    A. David defeats Goliath.
    B. At about your age David had a faith strong enough to make him risk his safety for his nation.
    C. The youth of today need such faith, for we live in difficult times with dangers all about; but let nothing shake your faith in God and in the triumph of right (1 John 5:4). The same faith is needed in classroom, business, athletic field, or battlefield.

II. Joseph, as a teenager, resisted temptation.
    A. Joseph is sold into slavery, but remains true.
    B. He went away from home under most adverse circumstances and if anyone had occasion to forget the God of his fathers, Joseph did.
    C. Yet when he was tempted, he would not yield but ran to defeat the temptation.
    D. If you would become what you hope to become, you must be able to withstand temptation—dishonesty, alcohol, immorality—do not think that such is a shortcut to what you want; it is a blind alley that will not get you there at all.

III. Esther, as a teenager (or just past), seized her opportunity to serve and acted.
    A. Esther risked her life to serve her people.
    B. Not many of us will have opportunities to save our whole nation at one great moment, but we all have opportunities daily to do good and to serve.

C. Whatever your walk in life, make it a way of serving.

Conclusion:

A. You have set your goals; I hope you can reach them.

B. If you reach these goals, however, you must have faith, resist temptation, and seize your opportunities.

ASSIGNMENT

Preaching for Special Occasions

Prepare for delivery in class either a wedding ceremony or a funeral sermon. If you prepare a wedding, include the vows as you would use them on the outline to be turned in, but you may stop your class presentation just before the giving of the vows. Again, give particular attention to style in this assignment, but give the speech extemporaneously. You may have worked on certain phrasing in advance, but the overall impression should be extemporaneous.

Additional reading on funeral and wedding sermons may be found in Chapter XXVI of George E. Sweazey's *Preaching the Good News* and Rex P. Kyker's *God's Man in Time of Death*.

Appendix

Listen to a recording of Peter Marshall's sermon, "Trumpet of the Morn" while watching this outline and explanation of techniques.

TRUMPET OF THE MORN

Purpose: **To stimulate the audience to greater faith, hope, and service.**

Introduction:

Quotation for attention	A. Mark 14:68.
Cases for attention	B. There are not many cities in the heart of which you may suddenly hear the crowing of a cock.
Note: the specific images by giving actual street locations	1. You cannot hear it in Washington, New York, Newark, Atlanta, Chicago, or Los Angeles.
	2. But you can hear it in Jerusalem.
Metaphor	"Trumpet of the dawn opened the flood gates of memory."

Hypothetical cases }

C. What would it do to young
people in a large city if they
were to hear a cock crow?

1. A young woman might hear
"bugle of the barnyard"

Metaphor }

2. A young man might hear. . . .

*Appeal to Convictions
Cases* }

D. God rescues in mysterious
ways.

Story for interest }

E. Last St. Andrews Day, I had an
unusual emotional experience.

*Note: Specific detail, active
words, and emotional
appeal to affections, social
approval, pleasure, con-
victions, self-preservation* }

F. Memories. How they come
surging back into the heart to
make it clean again or to accuse
it.

Body: Topical—(Narration with application for main headings)

*Story for interest
and to set stage for
application* }

I. But to Simon Peter, memory came in
the crowing of a cock.

A. Peter follows afar off.

*Specific detail
for imagery* }

"fists clinched, knuckles white,
veins standing out"

Simile }

"lanterns, like giant fireflies"

*Note: I. is arranged by
space as well as time* }

B. Peter came to the courtyard.

1. He entered with John.

2. He denies to the maid.

*After words "bugle call"
listen for build to climax,
then for gradual drop to a
pause after "eyes met."
Note pickup of speed
following the pause.* }

3. He warms by the fire.

4. He denies to the soldier.

5. He waits.

6. He denies to the soldier.

7. The cock crows.

8. He sees Jesus.

C. Peter runs to the porch.

1. The cock crows again.

2. He thinks long, long
thought.

3. He had remembered too late.

Striking phrase }
"saving memory"
"a blind rage was in the

Metaphor }
saddle"

Personification }
"tug of war"

D. Peter turned back from the porch.

II. Oh, if only we could speak to the men and the women standing on the porch today.

A. In the porch the danger lies.
B. There are many standing in the porch.

Note: Balanced phrase }
1. Some find the church of to day unattractive, insipid, in effective.

Signpost }
2. Others, tempted by the social standards of the pagan city, believe the church is

Metonymy—effect for cause }
out of step.
"pillow wet with tears"

Conclusion:
A. You may be standing on the porch.
1. Listen to the crowing of the cock.
2. You are a witness, you see.
a. You are witnessing something.

Not spoken }
b. Come help us.
c. (Do not be hindered by difficulties.)
(1) There are mysteries.
(a) Religious experi-

Metaphor }

Personification }

Quotation of poem }

Parallel statement }

Balanced phrase }

Note: parallel statement within both (b) and (c) as well as with each other }

Rhetorical question }

ence cannot always be poured into the cold, unsympathetic molds of speech.

(b) You cannot always give feet to the experiences that lie deepest in your heart.

(c) But do not be afraid of mysteries.

(d) While you may beware of the man who tries to explain everything, we must also beware of the man who insists upon having everything explained.

(2) There are difficulties in the way.

(a) We are not yet matching *our faith* with *our words.*

(b) Our greatest difficulty lies not in knowing what is God's will for our lives, but rather in being willing to do it. "Is it not yours also?"

(c) My problems with the Bible are not with the passages that I do not under-

Rhetorical question }   stand, but with the passages I do understand. "Is not that your problem?"

3. Let no one linger on the porch.
   a. You will deny Me, said Jesus, but you will "hear the birds of dawning crow."
   b. When a man hears that, he cannot linger on the porch.

Subject Sentence: Listen for the call that will summon you back to faith and hope and service. "And the cock crew and Peter remembered."

Transition
Appeal to convictions }   B. Wouldn't it be wonderful if today the cock would crow for you, and you, too, would remember.

Appeal to possessions }   1. Remember the vows you once made and the promises Christ made you.

Note: balanced phrases, under 2. }

Appeal to exploration }   2. With the return of these memories there could be the beginning of a new life.

Visualization for emotional appeal to respect and worship, convictions }   3. If the cock has crowed for you, you cannot stay on the porch; stand on Christ's side.

Appeal to self-preservation }   4. Watch, therefore.

Bibliography

Abbey, Merrill R. *Preaching to the Contemporary Mind.* New York: Abingdon Press, 1963.

Adams, Jay E. *Essays on Biblical Preaching.* Grand Rapids: Zondervan Publishing House, 1983.

_____ . *Preaching With Purpose.* Grand Rapids: Baker Book House, 1982.

Allen, Jimmy. "Christ, the Prince of Peace," *Great Sermons of 1967.* Austin: R. B. Sweet Publishing Co., 1967.

_____ . "To the Lifted Up Christ." *Abilene Christian College Annual Bible Lectures* (1965): 33.

Allen, Ronald J. *Preaching for Growth.* St. Louis: CBP Press, 1988.

Aristotle. *The Rhetoric of Aristotle.* Translated by Lane Cooper. New York: Appleton-Century-Crofts, 1932.

Bailey, Raymond. *Jesus the Preacher.* Nashville: Broadman Press, 1990.

_____ . *Paul the Preacher.* Nashville: Broadman Press, 1991.

Barth, Karl. *The Preaching of the Gospel.* Philadelphia: Westminster Press, 1963.

Baumann, J. Daniel. *An Introduction to Contemporary Preaching.* Grand Rapids: Baker Book House, 1972.

Baxter, Batsell Barrett. *The Heart of the Yale Lectures.* New York: Macmillan Co., 1947.

Beecher, Henry Ward. *Yale Lectures on Preaching.* New York: Charles Scribner's Sons, 1890.

Blackwood, Andrew W. *Biographical Preaching for Today.* Nashville: Abingdon Press, 1954.

————. *Doctrinal Preaching for Today.* Nashville: Abingdon Press, 1956.

————. *Expository Preaching for Today.* Nashville: Abingdon Press, 1953.

————. *Preaching from the Bible.* Nashville: Abingdon Press, 1941.

————. *The Preparation of Sermons.* Nashville: Abingdon-Cokesbury Press, 1948.

Braga, James. *How to Prepare Bible Messages.* Portland: Multinomah Press, 1981.

Broadus, John A. *On the Preparation and Delivery of Sermons.* Revised by J. B. Weatherspoon. New York: Harper & Row Publishers, 1944.

Brooks, Phillips. *Lectures on Preaching.* Grand Rapids: Zondervan Publishing House, n.d.

Bryant, Donald C., and Karl R. Wallace. *Fundamentals of Public Speaking.* 2d ed. New York: Appleton-Century-Crofts, 1953.

Bryson, Harold T., and James C. Taylor. *Building Sermons to Meet People's Needs.* Nashville: Zondervan, 1980.

Cannon, Jolen H., Jr. "The Power of Biblical Preaching." Doctoral thesis, Trinity Theological Seminary, 1984.

Chartler, Myron R. *Preaching as Communication*. Nashville: Abingdon, 1981.

Connel, Lloyd. *Christ in the Mountain and Other Sermons*. Oklahoma City: Telegram Book Co., 1960.

Cox, James W. *Preaching*. San Francisco: Harper & Row Publishers, 1985.

Craddock, Fred B. *Preaching*. Nashville: Abingdon Press, 1985.

Ehninger, Douglas, and Wayne Brockriede. *Decision by Debate*. New York: Dodd, Mead & Co., 1963.

Fant, Clyde. *Preaching for Today*. San Francisco: Harper & Row Publishers, 1987.

Freeman, Harold. *Variety in Biblical Preaching*. Waco: Word Books, 1987.

Gardner, Don. "To See Our Opportunities," *Abilene Christian College Annual Bible Lectures* (1965): 227.

Garrison, Webb B. *Creative Imagination in Preaching*. Nashville: Abingdon Press, 1960.

Gresham, Charles R., ed. *Preach the Word*. Joplin: College Press Publishing Co., 1983.

Hitchcock, Orville A. "Jonathan Edwards," *History and Criticism of American Public Address,* edited by William Norwood Brigance. New York: McGraw-Hill Book Co., Inc., 1943.

Hochmuth, Marie, and Norman W. Mattis. "Phillips Brooks," *A History and Criticism of American Public Address.* New York: McGraw-Hill Book Co., 1943.

Hybels, Bill, Stuart Briscoe, and Haddon Robinson. *Mastering Contemporary Preaching*. Portland: Multinomah Press, 1989.

Jackson, Edgar N. *How to Preach to People's Needs*. New York: Abingdon Press, 1956.

Jones, Ilian T. *Principles and Practice of Preaching*. Nashville: Abingdon Press, 1956.

Kennedy, Gerald. *His Word Through Preaching*. New York: Harper & Brother Publishers, 1947.

Kyker, Rex P. *God's Man in Time of Death*. Abilene, TX: ACU Bookstore, 1982.

Lantz, John Edward. *Speaking in the Church*. New York: Macmillan Co., 1954.

Lefan, James. "To Our Source of Help," *Abilene Christian College Annual Bible Lectures* (1965): 16, 17.

Lemmons, Reuel. "The Exceeding Sinfulness of Sin," *Great Sermons of 1967*. Austin: R. B. Sweet Publishing Co., 1967.

Lewis, Ralph L. *Speech for Persuasive Preaching*. Wilmore, KY: Asbury Theological Seminary, 1968.

Lewis, Ralph L., and Gregg Lewis. *Inductive Preaching: Helping People Listen*. Westchester, IL: Crossway Books, 1983.

Liefeld, Walter. *New Testament Exposition: From Text to Sermon*. Grand Rapids: Zondervan, 1984.

Long, Thomas G. *The Witness of Preaching*. Louisville: Westminster/John Knox Press, 1989.

McCall, Roy C. "Theodore Parker," *History and Criticism of American Public Address*. New York: McGraw-Hill Book Co., 1943.

Macartney, Clarence Edward. *Preaching Without Notes*. New York: Abingdon-Cokesbury Press, 1946.

McMillan, E. W. *The Minister's Spiritual Life*. Austin: Firm Foundation Publishing House, 1969.

McPherson, Ian. *The Art of Illustrating Sermons*. Nashville: Abingdon Press, 1964.

_____ . *The Burden of the Lord*. Nashville: Abingdon Press, 1955.

Meyer, Jack, Sr. *The Preacher and His Work*. Rev. and enl. ed. Athens, AL: The C.E.I. Store, 1960.

Monroe, Alan H. *Principles and Types of Speech*. 3d ed. New York: Scott, Foresman and Co., 1949.

Pack, Frank, and Prentice Meador. *Preaching to Modern Man*. Abilene, TX: Biblical Research Press, 1969.

Pattison, T. Harwood. *The Making of the Sermon*. Philadelphia: American Baptist Publication Society, 1951.

Quintilian. *The Institutio Oratoria*. Translated by H. H. Butler. Cambridge, MA: Harvard University Press, 1921-22.

Richardson, Robert. *Memoirs of Alexander Campbell*. Cincinnati: Standard Publishing Co., 1897.

Robinson, George L. "Historical and Scriptural Digest," *The Master Bible*. Indianapolis: J. Wesley Dickson & Co., 1947.

Robinson, Haddon W. *Biblical Preaching: The Development and Delivery of Expository Messages*. Grand Rapids: Baker Book House, 1980.

Sanders, J. Pliant, C. Arthur Norred, Fanning Yater Tant, and Roy E. Cogdill. *Preaching in the Twentieth Century*. Los Angeles: Old Paths Book Club, 1945.

Sangster, W. E. *The Craft of Sermon Illustration*. Philadelphia: Westminster Press, 1950.

Smith, Foy L. *The World Is Yours and Other Sermons*. Oklahoma City: Telegram Book Co., 1959.

Stott, John R. W. *The Preacher's Portrait*. Grand Rapids: Wm. B. Eerdmans Publishing Co., 1961.

_____ . *Between Two Worlds: The Art of Preaching in the Twentieth Century*. Grand Rapids: Wm. B. Eerdmans Publishing Co., 1982.

Sweazey, George E. *Preaching the Good News.* Englewood Cliffs, N.J.: Prentice Hall, 1976.

Thayer, Joseph Henry. *A Greek-English Lexicon of the New Testament.* New York: American Book Co., 1889.

Thomas, D. *The Biblical Illustrator.* Edited by Joseph S. Excell, St. John. Grand Rapids: Baker Book House, 1953.

Toohey, William, and William D. Thompson, eds. *Recent Homiletical Thought: A Bibliography, 1935-1965.* New York: Abingdon Press, 1967.

Walker, Granville T. *Preaching in the Thought of Alexander Campbell.* St. Louis: The Bethany Press, 1967.

Wardlaw, Don M., ed. *Preaching Biblically: Creating Sermons Shape of Scripture.* Philadelphia: Westminster Press, 1983.

Whitesell, Faris D. *Power in Expository Preaching.* Westwood, N.J.: Fleming H. Revell Co., 1963.

Yates, Kyle M. *Preaching from the Prophets.* Nashville: Broadman Press, 1942.

Index